I NEED A J-O-B!

The Ex-offender's Job Search Manual

Louis N. Jones

CONQUEST BOOKS

I NEED A J-O-B!
The Ex-Offender's Job Search Manual
Published by Conquest Publications
A division of ConquestHouse, Inc.
PO Box 73873
Washington, DC 20056-3873

Copyright 2003, 2005 ConquestHouse, Inc.

ISBN: 0-9656625-2-7

Printed in the United States of America

Scripture quotations ending with the abbreviation (NASB) taken from the New American Standard Bible Copyrighted © 1960, 1962, 1963, 1968, 1971, 1972, 1973, 1975, 1977, by the Lockman Foundation. Used by permission.

Scripture quotations ending with the abbreviation (NIV) excerpted from *Compton's Interactive Bible NIV*. Copyrighted © 1994, 1995, 1996 SoftKey Multimedia Inc. All Rights Reserved.

CONQUEST
BOOKS

"All labor that uplifts humanity has dignity and importance and should be undertaken with painstaking excellence."

Dr. Martin Luther King Jr.
American Civil Rights Leader

"If a man is called to be a street sweeper, he should sweep streets even as Michelangelo painted, or Beethoven played music, or Shakespeare wrote poetry. He should sweep streets so well that all the hosts of heaven and earth will pause to say, here lived a great street sweeper who did his job well."

Martin Luther King Jr.
American Civil Rights Leader

Contents

Preface

In beginning this book, I wish to point out one fact that is obvious to any man or woman who has spent more than a year in prison.

Being an ex-offender looking for work is *hard*.

I don't mean difficult. I mean hard. Hard as in gut-wrenching struggle, unflinching. I want to acknowledge that early, because I do not want you to think that what I am about to present is an easy get-a-job course. Unless you happen to be a graduate of Harvard University and routinely bump shoulders with executives at Fortune 500 corporations, finding a job may not be easy. As an ex-offender looking for work, you may find it to be quite difficult.

If you look at the factors against ex-offenders finding work, it is easy to become discouraged. Some employers will not hire ex-offenders, regardless of what they have done, because they do not want to be sued for negligent hiring practices. Others will hire ex-offenders convicted of certain offenses but not others. In many states, it is legal to deny an ex-offender employment based on his criminal record. In addition, many ex-offenders have limited social, vocational, and life skills, which are needed to find employment and keep it. Many ex-offenders have never held a regular job before imprisonment.

Further complicating the problem is the slow economy and the increasingly intensive competition for the low-wage, low-skill jobs that many ex-offenders are eligible for. No wonder many ex-offenders throw up their hands, give up, and return to criminal activity.

This book is written for the ex-offender who has or will be facing the daunting search for employment. For many of you, employment is not an option, because you have to remain employed to avoid a technical violation of your parole and a return to prison. You may have a family to support. On the other hand, you may not have anyone to support other than yourself. Whatever the situation, one thing is clear: if you want to remain out of prison and become successful, getting and keeping a job should be your number-one priority.

This book is designed to provide you with information and advice that will empower you to perform an effective job search. Truthfully, you may get lucky and find a job without following the advice in this book. However, if you want to increase the chances of finding work, put yourself in the best position to find job openings, nail that interview, and get hired, this book contains practical tips on how to proceed.

What this book will not do is *guarantee* that you will get a job. Whether you get a job depends on your willingness and your commitment to finding work despite the obstacles. This is not *an easy way to a job* manual. There are some suggestions in this book, and while reading them, you may wonder, "Why do I have to do all that?" But remember, successful people are those who are willing to take the time and work to accomplish their goals. They do not depend on luck or chance. If you want to find a job, you cannot wait for one to fall out of the sky. This book is a guide for the effort you will have to put in to find the job that is waiting for you.

Support Beyond This Book

The suggestions contained in this book are meant to provide you with solid guidance for finding a job in today's difficult job market. But probably the most important piece of advice I am going to give in this book is contained within this chapter.

The job search can be frustrating and draining. You may feel that you have to do it alone, and there is no one around who can help.

But, as an ex-offender looking for work, you will need support. You cannot do it all by yourself. You will need someone in your life to hold you accountable and to help encourage you to keep on going despite the odds. And while there are some encouraging words within the pages of this book, the most powerful encouragement can come from someone with whom you have a relationship. And as much as I would like this not to be true, you cannot build a relationship with a publication.

As a minister of the gospel, I need support as well. Life is filled with many obstacles and discouraging events that can easily draw me down and get me depressed and despondent. That is the case with all of us. Whatever your challenge, there will be times when you need the support of someone stronger than you, someone to hold you accountable.

I would like to recommend someone who can provide you with that support. His name is Jesus Christ.

Through a personal relationship with Jesus Christ, you can have clarity, focus, and strength like you have never had before. I am not talking about going to church, sitting in the pews, listening to a sermon every Sunday, and then calling yourself a Christian. I am talking about taking it one step further by submitting yourself to His will and acknowledging His word. There is a life that is more fulfilling than any life you can hope to achieve by getting quick money, getting high, or gaining massive mounts of power and control over others. I am speaking of a life of peace, prosperity, happiness, and the restoration of your life back to God's divine and ordained purpose.

I urge you to review and follow the *Steps to Peace with God* listed below.

steps to peace with God

Step One
God's Purpose: Peace and Life

God loves you and wants you to experience peace and life—abundant and eternal.

The Bible says...

"We have peace with God through our Lord Jesus Christ." Romans 5:1

"For God so loved the world that He gave His only begotten Son, that whoever believes in Him should not perish but have everlasting life." John 3:16

"I have come that they may have life, and that they may have it more abundantly." John 10:10

Why don't most people have this peace and abundant life that God planned for us to have?

Step Two
The Problem: Our Separation

God created us in His own image to have an abundant life. He did not make us as robots to automatically love and obey Him. God gave us a will and a freedom of choice.

We chose to disobey God and go our own willful way. We still make this choice today. This results in separation from God.

The Bible says...

"For all have sinned and fall short of the glory of God." Romans 3:23

"For the wages of sin is death, but the gift of God is eternal life in Christ Jesus our Lord." Romans 6:23

Our Attempts to Reach God

People have tried in many ways to bridge this gap between themselves and God.

The Bible says...

"There is a way that seems right to a man, but in the end it leads to death." Proverbs 14:12

"But your iniquities have separated you from your God; your sins have hidden his face from you, so that he will not hear." Isaiah 59:2

No bridge reaches God—except one.

Step Three
God's Bridge: The Cross

Jesus Christ died on the Cross and rose from the grave. He paid the penalty for our sin and bridged the gap between God and people.

The Bible says...

"For there is one God and one mediator between God and men, the man Jesus Christ." 1 Timothy 2:5

"For Christ died for sins once for all, the righteous for the unrighteous, to bring you to God." 1 Peter 3:18

"But God demonstrates his own love for us in this: While we were still sinners, Christ died for us." Romans 5:8

God has provided the only way. Each person must make a choice.

Step Four
Our Response: Receive Christ

We must trust Jesus Christ as Lord and Savior and receive Him by personal invitation.

The Bible says...

"Here I am! I stand at the door and knock. If anyone hears my voice and opens the door, I will come in and eat with him, and he with me." Revelation 3:20

"Yet to all who received him, to those who believed in his name, he gave the right to become children of God." John 1:12

"That if you confess with your mouth, 'Jesus is Lord,' and believe in your heart that God raised Him from the dead, you will be saved." Romans 10:9

Where are you?

Will you receive Jesus Christ right now?

Here is how you can receive Christ:

1. Admit your need. (I am a sinner.)
2. Be willing to turn from your sins. (Repent.)
3. Believe that Jesus Christ died for you on the Cross and rose from the grave.
4. Through prayer, invite Jesus Christ to come in and control your life through the Holy Spirit. (Receive Him as Lord and Savior.)

How to Pray:

Dear Lord Jesus,

I know that I am a sinner and need Your forgiveness. I believe that You died for my sins. I want to turn from my sins. I now invite You to come into my heart and life. I want to trust and follow You as Lord and Savior.

In Jesus' name. Amen.

God's Assurance: His Word

If you prayed this prayer,

The Bible says...

"Everyone who calls on the name of the Lord will be saved." Romans 10:13

Did you sincerely ask Jesus Christ to come into your life? Where is He right now? What has He given you?

"For it is by grace you have been saved, through faith—and this not from yourselves, it is the gift of God—not by works, so that no one can boast." Ephesians 2:8–9

Receiving Christ, we are born into God's family through the supernatural work of the Holy Spirit who dwells in every believer. This is called regeneration, or the "new birth."

This is just the beginning of a wonderful new life in Christ. To deepen this relationship you should:

1. Read your Bible everyday to know Christ better.
2. Talk to God in prayer every day.
3. Tell others about Christ.
4. Worship, fellowship, and serve with other Christians in a church where Christ is preached.
5. As Christ's representative in a needy world, demonstrate your new life by your love and concern for others.

BENEFITS OF EMPLOYMENT

We know that in this economy-driven country, the one prevailing benefit of employment

is getting *paid*. However, if that is all a job means to you, then you are missing the mark. There are many benefits of employment other than the pleasure of being compensated for what you do. Here, we want to broaden your view of employment as more than just a means to get money. So, we will ignore the obvious, and focus on the not-so-obvious benefits to finding a job in a good company.

Benefit #1: Employment cuts down on idle time and makes your life productive.
There is much truth in the adage "an idle mind is the devil's workshop." It is dangerous to spend all of your time doing nothing productive, just as it is dangerous to spend all of your time working. Life should be a comfortable balance between work, play, and rest. When that balance is disrupted, life becomes miserable, and we try to find ways to ease or end that misery.

Humans have a natural need to do something. If that were not the case, we would sleep most of our lives. We want our lives to be about something, to be productive. Our need to *do* can be positive or negative. If we do not engage in positive activities, we will surely engage in negative ones. For anyone who does not work and does not engage in any positive productive activity, the mind and heart become open to the negative stuff.

For those who have committed crimes, there is always a strong pull toward the negative.

A story in the Bible illustrates this. In Matthew 12:43–45, Jesus said:

When an evil spirit leaves a person, it goes into the desert, seeking rest but finding none. Then it says, 'I will return to the person I came from.' So it returns and finds its former home empty, swept, and clean. Then the spirit finds seven other spirits more evil than itself, and they all enter the person and live there. And so that person is worse off than before. That will be the experience of this evil generation.

An ex-offender returning from prison is a lot like the former home of an evil spirit. The ex-offender is out of prison, supposedly "rehabilitated," and has paid his debt. He is as a house that is empty, swept, and clean. And he is also a prime target for the evil spirit to return, live there, and make him worse than he was before.

Washington, DC, has many vacant properties. Many of these properties have been abandoned or ignored by their owners. Many of these buildings have become magnets for drug dealers, prostitutes, and others. Such is the destiny of an empty home that has not been filled.

If you want to stay out of prison, you must fill your life with activities that yield positive fruit. Employment is a positive activity that can improve your financial health, fill those idle hours, and leave less time for pondering the negative.

Benefit #2. Employment improves your social status.

Have you ever heard a person trying to describe he is unemployed by using the phrase "I'm between jobs"? That phrase sounds much better, and makes you feel much better. Yet it does not change the fact that you do not have a job, and probably have no immediate prospects for a new one.

The reason such phrases are used is because being unemployed in this country is like being at the bottom of the social-economic ladder. As I write this, 5.2 percent of the U S population is "between jobs" (and that's just the ones who have filed for unemployment). If you one of the 5.2 percent, many people may look down on you and wonder what is so wrong with you that you cannot find a job. They may think you are lazy or a poor worker. You witness all your friends talking about their jobs, making plans. In addition, if you are a man and happen to have found that special sweetheart, telling her you do not have a job may cause her to hop on the first train heading out of your life. Face it. Not having a job puts you at the bottom of the social ladder, and probably makes you a babysitter for all of your employed friends' kids.

So, for all those friends who snapped, "get a job!" every time you asked for a few bucks, put them to shame. Employment improves your social status and your self-esteem.

Benefit #3: Employment improves your stock of personal and business relationships.

As an ex-offender, one of the last things you want to do is hang around with negative friends. Spending time in positive places such as on a job or in church can put you in contact with friends who can help to improve your life rather than destroy it. In addition, by having a job, you can increase the number of references you have, which will be useful if you are looking for a better job or going into business for yourself. Having a job is a good place for networking and making contacts in your chosen field or profession.

Benefit #4: Employment can be a tremendous training ground.

Experience is the best teacher. One of the best ways of learning how to do something is to do it. Getting a regular job puts you on a wonderful training ground. If you are open to learning, there are many lessons that can be taught just by doing your job. Among them:

1) Learning how to follow instructions
2) Learning on-the-job vocational skills
3) Learning how to be on time
4) Being patient
5) Becoming responsible
6) Juggling tasks
7) Becoming organized

For instance, many people tell me I am an organized person. But I didn't just wake up one day and decide to be organized. It was something that I learned over a few years of working in office environments. It was there I learned how to file and learned all about filing systems. I learned about calendars, recording appointments, Rolodexes, and all the other trappings of office organization. I use many of these same principles in my personal life. Therefore, I learned how to be organized by watching it being done on the job.

Having a job can enrich you in many areas, broaden your horizons, and may give you an education you may not have had. In addition, if you do not have a skill, you can often learn one by taking on a job where there is an apprentice program or on-the-job training program.

Benefit #5. Employment improves your independence.
If you do not have a job and no income, then you are always dependent on others for your survival. Everything you need—food, clothes, shelter—depends on someone else having to get those for you. And I have yet to speak to any adult who enjoys being dependent on others for his daily needs.

When kids become teenagers and move on into adulthood, they relish the idea of being independent of their parents, doing their own thing, having their own money, and taking care of themselves. It is one of the hallmarks of adulthood. We go on and take care of ourselves.

Unfortunately, imprisonment often abruptly ends many of the responsibilities and independence of adulthood. Many of the decisions that most free people take for granted are removed from the prisoner. Unfortunately, this status often continues on release, with the ex-offender being dependent on others for everything. After a long prison sentence, this may be all he is used to doing, and it may be difficult to adopt a lifestyle of taking care of himself. This perpetuates the lack of freedom that is experienced in prison, and takes a tremendous toll on the ex-offender's self-esteem.

Employment is a symbol of independence. Many people not only want jobs but also want jobs where they can break all financial and material dependence on others and can begin to take care of themselves and others in their lives. This is especially important for men, whose self-esteem and self-confidence are inherently connected to their ability to provide for themselves and their families.

Benefit #6. If you are on parole or probation, a good steady job almost always eases the worry of your supervisory officer.

Your parole or probation officer's primary job is to make sure that you remain a law-abiding citizen while you are on the streets. The supervisory officer is there to protect the public interest. One of the primary indicators of a potential return to crime is lack of a job. So, if you do not have a job, and you do not have a good reason for not having one, you could be considered a risk to public safety and be sanctioned by your supervisory officer. Such sanctions could include a return to prison.

I once heard an ex-offender tell me that he was going to make his supervisory officer "mad" by doing everything right, by getting a job, and by keeping himself out of trouble. To him, the supervisory officer lives for the moment when the ex-offender screws up. Actually, the opposite is true. Since the officer's job is to keep his charges from committing criminal activity, if you get a job and stay out of trouble, you may become one of the officer's favorite charges. He knows that if you are employed and making money, you are less likely to commit any new crimes. Most supervisory officers are not masochists—they want to see you succeed. Getting a job would make life easier on your officer, and make life easier on you too.

Having presented you with the benefits of employment, it is my hope that you have determined that getting a job is not optional. It is necessary to improve your life, successfully reintegrate into society, and put the pain of the past farther and farther behind you. If you are able to work, it should become a top priority in your life, and you should be willing to extend whatever energies or resources you have to ensure that you get a job.

So, get ready for battle. Suit up, and prepare to fight. The battle is yours, if you are willing to remain steadfast until the end. A Scripture of note (Hebrews 12:1–2): *Wherefore seeing we also are compassed about with so great a cloud of witnesses, let us lay aside every weight, and the sin which doth so easily beset [us], and let us run with patience the race that is set before us, Looking unto Jesus the author and finisher of [our] faith; who for the joy that was set before him endured the cross, despising the shame, and is set down at the right hand of the throne of God.*

Knowing The Enemy

You noticed that I have abruptly switched to a battle mentality. This is because for an ex-offender, the road of finding a job is beset with many enemies and often feels like a game of tug-of-war. To fight a good battle, you must know your enemies and what to expect from them: understand that they are sneaky and underhanded and will try to catch you off-guard. Many times when you think you are so close to finding a job, they will creep in. They may pop up as soon as you look for a job. They may pop up before you look for a job. They may be present right now as you read this book. You need to be able to wage a good offense and put up a good defense.

The famous book by Sun Tzu, *The Art of War*, contains the following passage, as translated by Samuel B. Griffith:

31. Therefore I say: 'Know the enemy and know yourself; in a hundred battles you will never be in peril.

32. When you are ignorant of the enemy but know yourself, your chances of winning or losing are equal.

33. If ignorant both of your enemy and of yourself, you are certain in every battle to be in peril.'

So, what are the enemies of your job search? What factors are out there preventing you from getting a job? Here are a few you may be thinking of:
- ➢ **The Economy and Lack of Jobs**
- ➢ **Racism**
- ➢ **Employer Apathy (Lack of interest)**
- ➢ **Laws and Policies Preventing Offender Access To Employment**

Yes, these are enemies. They are out there, preventing you from finding a job. Throughout your job search, you will have to deal with them. However, these deeply entrenched soldiers are the ones guarding the fortress. They are powerful enemies, and you will not be able to handle them alone. Dealing with these enemies takes a systematic approach involving strategies and methods that are not within the scope of this book.

However, there are also front-line soldiers: they are likely to be the first ones you meet. They will often keep you from getting anywhere near the fortress. Once you get through them, you have won your first battle. They are:

> **Rejection**
> **Frustration**
> **Laziness**
> **Fatigue**
> **Lack of Positive Self-Esteem**

Let's look at each and see how you can defeat them.

REJECTION

Rejection is a part of every job search, whether you are an ex-offender or not. Yet, it is also one of the most difficult aspects of finding a job. After you have applied for ten to twelve jobs, and you have been told "no" ten to twelve times, it can take its toll.

Rejection can be either *direct* or *subtle*. *Direct rejection* is when you get a letter or a phone call from the employer telling you that you did not get the job. Subtle rejection is when you have called 900 times inquiring about the position, and no one returns your call. No one has told you no or yes, but you can tell from the cold shoulder there is no chance of getting that job.

The aim of this enemy is to gang up on you, hand you ten to twelve rejections, and get you feeling that because they reject you, everyone else will reject you. They know that after hearing so many rejections, it will take an emotional toll on you, and you just simply do not want to hear it any more. Therefore, you give up.

DO NOT GIVE UP! Rejection is a part of life, and, if you want to find a job, you cannot take rejection personally. Most books that are published were rejected several times before a publisher decided to print them. Some of the most successful movies you see at the theater were shopped around from studio to studio before someone bought them.

A point to ponder: *.Being rejected does not necessarily mean that what you have to offer is not good.*

Twice the high school basketball team rejected Michael Jordan before the coach agreed to let him try.

Coca-Cola only sold 400 bottles in its first year. That is a failure by many standards. Now it is one of the best-selling soft drinks in the world.

Margaret Mitchell, author of *Gone With The Wind*, received twenty-five rejection letters before a publisher accepted the book, never knowing it would be a classic.

You are likely to have the same experience. But keep on looking. Eventually someone will send you an offer letter, and all those rejections will melt away like a snowball on a Florida sidewalk.

FRUSTRATION

Frustration is the feeling similar to that you would get if you tried to ride a bicycle through a solid brick wall. No matter what you try, you just can't get through, and you're never going to go anywhere.

The key to dealing with frustration is to recognize there may be several ways of reaching the same goal. With the bicyclist above, he is frustrated because he cannot get through the brick wall. But what about riding around it? Climbing over it? Getting someone or something stronger than himself and knocking it down?

When you feel frustrated, that is not the time to give up. That is the time to examine your approach and determine if your goal of finding a job can be accomplished another way. And even if there isn't another way, we should not give up on what it is we are trying to do. You never know. At some point, something may come along and knock down that wall for you. But if you've given up, you'll never reap the benefits.

Life is full of frustration. Sometimes we make plans, and they go awry. The question is, will we give up or will we adapt?

Have you ever tried to put a three-prong cord into a two-prong electrical outlet? No matter how much you force it, it just will not fit. You could pull out the third prong, but that will destroy the function of the cord. On the other hand, you could buy a small device with three holes on one end and two prongs on the other. This adaptor changes the cord without changing its function, so it can fit into the outlet.

When we are faced with frustration, we need to be open to change and have the ability to adapt to the circumstance. Part of adapting means not developing unrealistic expectations. So many ex-offenders get frustrated because they expect to get a job in two to three weeks. It is not unusual to spend six months or more looking for employment.

Rejection often leads to frustration in the job search. The key is not to give up, but to continue to move forward. Great dreamers never give up on their dreams, even if they think they will not be the ones to see it.

"Nothing in the world can take the place of persistence. Talent will not; nothing in the world is more common than unsuccessful men with talent. Genius will not; unrewarded genius is a proverb. Education will not; the world is full of educated derelicts. Persistence and determination alone are omnipotent..."

LAZINESS

If you really want to find a job, then laziness will not be your best friend. The job search will involve work. It will involve diligence. It will involve follow-up. If your idea of a job search is to spend most of the week lying around in front of the TV and pursuing one or two job leads a week, it is going to be a long time before someone says, "You're hired!"

Those who are successful in their job search make finding a job in itself a full-time job. They are up at 7 a.m., making phone calls, filling out applications, pursuing leads, checking the want ads. They do not relax and wait for the phone to ring. They are not draw by the temptation of relaxing during most of their free time. You will rarely find them at home during the business day, because they are out looking for work.

There is a subculture in our society today in which ease and convenience is the order of the day. People are seeking products and programs that will remove as much work from their lives as possible. Every time I go to the grocery store, I see a new convenience food. These options even exist in the employment search world. Employment agencies, however well meaning, take the legwork out of finding a job by finding employers for you. If you use the services of an employment agency, you may feel as if you do not need to go out and look for a job—that the employment agency should "find" you a job.

In fact, most good employment agencies will work with you and tell you some of the same things we are telling you in this book. They may have a few job leads, but you should not rely on those leads alone. To maximize your job search and increase your chances of finding employment, an employment agency should be only one of the weapons in your arsenal. You will still need to hit the streets. You will still need to check the want ads. You will still need to employ all the other principles we will tell you about later. There is no substitute for good old-fashioned work.

FATIGUE

Of course, being a hard worker at a job search does not mean you have to do it twenty-four hours a day, seven days a week. The job search can be tedious as well as physically and emotionally draining. Pounding the pavement (especially in hot weather), only to hear several rejections a week, can take its toll on anyone. Just as important as being hard-working and diligent in your job search is knowing when to rest and free your body and mind from the stress of the experience. You do not want to wear yourself out.

Only you can determine your threshold. If you have been working hard at the job search, and you feel yourself becoming tired and stressed out, take a day off. Being tired and stressed out can affect your attitude, and you need a good attitude during the job search. Once fatigue sets in, you are also prone to making mistakes and cutting corners.

You should also make sure you get the needed amount of sleep at night. Between six and eight hours a night is suggested. (Most health experts have found that the average person needs eight hours of sleep a night.) So, during your job search, you want to restrict or limit any activities that will keep you up at night and prevent you from getting the proper amount of rest. Remember, looking for a job is a job itself. As with any job, you need the proper sleep to function properly and perform your required duties.

LACK OF POSITIVE SELF-ESTEEM

Self-esteem is the way a person thinks and feels about himself and how well he does things that are important to him. Lack of positive self-esteem is a very powerful enemy that often afflicts those with criminal backgrounds. It is likely that you may have adopted the same feelings about yourself that society feels about you. It is likely that guilt and shame have overcome you, and you feel that you are not going to be of any good use to anyone. If any of the following applies to you, it is likely you may have a lack of positive self-esteem:

➤ Feeling that you are not good or worthy enough for anyone to employ
➤ Feeling that you will lose the job the moment you get one
➤ Feeling that you are a bad or evil person and that you will never change
➤ Feeling that you have nothing to contribute to society
➤ Thoughts of suicide
➤ Feeling that crime is the only thing you can do well
➤ Inability to go to church or pray or seek God because of guilt and shame
➤ Thinking that you are ugly, or too fat, or other lack of confidence about your body image
➤ Lack of education or illiteracy
➤ Physical or mental disability
➤ Feeling at a disadvantage because of your race

While it is not within the scope of this book to address each individual area of self-esteem, you should seek counseling from a minister or other professional to help you work through these issues if any apply. I will, however, offer a few of my own thoughts.

You are a human being. You are subject to mistakes and failure. You are subject to doing stupid things that you know you should not have done. None of us is immune.

However, the real mistake is to think of yourself entirely in light of your past errors. While you may have done some things in the past that you shouldn't have, God created you for something special.

Many people in society do not subscribe to that thinking. They want to hold that crime over you for the rest of your life. Because they cannot trust you, they assume that you cannot change and will not change. So, you are blacklisted and considered a criminal for life.

It is essential that you do not think about yourself the way they think about you. Deep down inside all the hurt and the struggle, there is a decent human being waiting to get out. With some counseling, you can find that person. There are ways to shed the pain of the past and become, as the Bible declares, "a new creation in Christ Jesus."

Changing how you think about yourself is essential for finding a job. After all, you will need to convince employers that you are worthy to be hired. If you do not believe this yourself, then you will have a hard time getting others to believe it. A positive self-esteem is reflected in your image and the way you present yourself. So is negative self-esteem.

This does not mean that you should think more of yourself than you ought to. I want to caution you against arrogance. A positive self-esteem means that you feel good about yourself, even though you make mistakes. No matter how good you are, there is always someone who is better than you. So, it is just as wrong to go out looking for jobs feeling like the companies to which you apply for jobs need you more than they need anyone else. They can do without you. You have to recognize that and present yourself as a good worker who can improve the employer's business, even though you have your faults.

Knowing Yourself

You have been introduced to your enemies who can hinder your job search. Now it is time to get to know yourself.

This involves finding out what you can do and what you cannot do. This involves knowing your skills, interests, what ticks you off, what doesn't, the work environment you are most comfortable in, the people you are most comfortable with, etc. This involves performing a self-assessment to find out what career is best for you and has the greatest potential for success.

I know. You just want a job. You'll do anything at this point, because you just want to feed yourself and your family. Ex-offenders often do not have many job options, so why do you have to limit yourself?

It is true that you may be willing to do anything at this point, as long as it pays money. I have often had ex-offenders approach me about finding a job. When I asked them what they could do, some of them have told me "I can do anything." But, you cannot do *anything*. No one can. Your ability to find a job and keep it involves knowing what it is you can do *well* so you can effectively channel your job search and present those skills to an employer. Knowing what you can *do well* and knowing what you *enjoy doing* increases your confidence during interviews, which will lead to a more effective interview. *Knowing yourself* is the key to finding a good job.

I am not suggesting that you limit yourself to one career choice. Ex-offenders need as many choices as they can get. But for every career path that you choose, however many they may be, the key is making sure the one you choose is right for you.

People are motivated most by what they enjoy. If you are going after a career path that you dislike, you may find a job initially, but you will never last for long. In addition, if you are pursuing a career path that does not fit you, the temptation to give up is a lot stronger.

So, how do you know what you career paths will be? What types of jobs should you target in your job search? Let's start by assessing the following areas:

Personality

Webster's definition of the word "personality": *The totality of qualities and traits, as of character or behavior, that are peculiar to an individual.*

Every human being on the planet Earth has a unique fingerprint, with a design that no one else has.

Similarly, you also have a unique set of qualities and traits, known as your personality. God created you to be a unique individual, different from everyone else on the planet, yet having enough in common that we can live in solidarity with one another.

It is not enough to try to adopt someone else's personality. God gave you one of your own. It is your responsibility to discover that uniqueness that God placed in you, and for you to conduct your life in accordance with what God has placed in you.

I believe that the key is discovering not yourself, but discovering God and His plans for your life.

Many people's personalities have been shaped by their life experiences and circumstances rather than God. Unfortunately, many ex-offenders have had experiences in life that are negative and thus lead to negative qualities and behavior.

Knowing your personality can help you determine what types of jobs you are most suited for. Not everyone is suited to work in an office environment; not everyone can be a construction worker. Knowing the type of person you are, your interests and dislikes, what drives you, what makes you upset, etc. can help you target those jobs where you will see the greatest potential for success. Your personality, in conjunction with the other areas listed below, can help you determine the most appropriate career path.

I regress. You're an ex-offender. You just need *a job*. Why go through all of this?

Many ex-offenders are encouraged to get whatever job they can. And I do not disagree. But many ex-offenders are done a tremendous disservice by simply being pushed into jobs for which they may be inadequate, ill-suited, or unqualified. As a result, they are unmotivated by what they are doing and are far more likely to quit. By channeling your job search to a career that is best suited for you, you will be more motivated to pursue it and keep it. Of course, you should always keep other options open.

We recommend you sit down with a minister, employment counselor, or other counselor to determine which line of work best suits your personality.

Skills and Natural Abilities

Skills come to us either through training or naturally. For instance, some people are taught to sing, while others have a natural knack for it from childhood. Take a piece of paper and list the skills and abilities that you possess that could be used in an employment setting.

Knowledge

Knowledge is information acquired through *experience* or *education*. What do you know that could be used in a job setting? For instance, many people's experiences in prison and the criminal justice system have made them effective counselors for ex-offenders. Or your knowledge of the streets could make you an effective law enforcement official. Or, while you were in prison, if you studied the Bible and learned many Scriptures, you may be an effective minister or evangelist. Often, people without many skills are hired for the wealth of information and knowledge that they possess, so do not discount the knowledge you have developed through your life's experiences.

On the same piece of paper that you listed your skills, detail the knowledge you have that could be helpful on a job.

Hobbies

Hobbies are those activities that people do that they immensely enjoy. Some people do not like to turn hobbies into careers because it destroys the sense of fun and turns the hobby into work, rather than play. However, many people have taken their hobbies and turned them into full-time careers and find that they enjoy them. Whether you want to keep your hobbies sacred or turn them into careers is up to you. Should you decide to seek a career related to one or more of your hobbies, the skill level needed to perform a hobby in a work environment may be greater than performing it unsupervised in your basement at home. Be honest with yourself and make sure that you are thoroughly skilled before going in this direction. Nonetheless, on a piece of paper, list your hobbies.

Health

Despite your knowledge, skills, and abilities, and need to pursue a particular career, there is one area that could overrule all of those considerations—your health. Simply speaking, if you are not in good mental or physical health, you are going to be limited as to the jobs you can perform. An honest assessment of your health and your ability to perform jobs could be important in not only whether you get a job, but whether you are able to keep it.

A question that almost every employer asks on a job application goes something like this: "Do you have any health issues that could prevent you from effectively performing your job?" Some applications will even list certain diseases or ailments and ask you to check off all those you are suffering from. The intent of this is for the employer to avoid hiring people who may not be able to perform their jobs because of their health issues. Many people will deny any health concerns, simply because they believe their health is none of the employer's business.

In fact, it is the employer's business. He understands the job environment more than you, and he wants to make sure that he is not hiring someone and placing him into a work environment that could be harmful to you or the other employers. For instance, if you have foot problems and cannot stand for long periods of time, it may not be a good idea to apply for a job in construction. Or, if you are allergic to dust, a cleaning job may not be ideal.

Employers have to be careful with this, however. There are federal and state laws forbidding discrimination against those who are physically or mentally disabled. So, an employer is likely to be careful in denying employment to someone based on his or her health. If the employer denies someone a job based on health concerns, the employer must be able to prove that the denial was because the health concern would prevent the job seeker from effectively performing his job. Employers are under no obligation to hire you if your health prevents you from adequately performing the job.

So, be honest with yourself and the employers. Take an inventory of any health issues you have, particularly those that require regular care from health professionals or require medication.

Experience

Experience is the measure of practice you have had in applying a particular skill and ability. Employers are not just looking for people who have a particular skill; they are looking for people who can show a track record of applying that skill in a work environment.

So with all of your skills and abilities you have listed, list how many months or years of experience you have had applying that skill.

Selecting the Job that is Right

Having assessed your personality, skills, knowledge, hobbies, health, and experience, you are ready to decide what jobs you will focus on. To do that, you will need to know what jobs are available in your community.

The easiest way to do this is to get a copy of your local newspaper and scan the want ads. The jobs that are listed more than any other are the jobs that you want check out to find out if your qualifications fit the position. Jobs that are available will vary from community to community. Some cities and communities are heavily industrial in nature, so they will have more factory-type jobs. Others are heavily technological, and will have plenty of computer-related positions. Use the newspaper and other job-related publications in your area to determine what jobs are available and what these jobs are paying.

Unfortunately, your skills may not match with the jobs available. For example, if you come out of prison with cooking skills, and you come back home to a community where there is only one restaurant within forty miles, you may not find many jobs using the skills you have. Therefore, you have the following choices:

1) Continue to look for a job that fits you, knowing that it may take a while to find something.
2) Take a job that does not fit you, but allows you to pay the bills.
3) Take training to learn the skills most needed in your community.
4) Move to a community where there is a great demand for your skills.
5) Which of these options you decide to take is up to you, and depends on your individual situation. But before relying on the above options, you will want to research the job market in your area and find out which jobs fit the skills and abilities you have.

If there is a reputable jobs counselor in your area, this may be a good time to seek him or her out. A jobs counselor has knowledge of the labor market and can help you decide what direction to take with a career choice. You can find a jobs counselor by calling information in your area and asking for the city or state employment office, or by going to the Career One-Stop on the Internet, located at www.careeronestop.org.

Of course, you may be desperate, and will take any paying job that anyone hands you at this point, whether you're suited to it or not. If that is your situation, then please do so. But do not end your job search there. Even if you already have a job, you can still begin a job search and follow the advice I give in this chapter. It is worth it to ensure that your next job is not only one that pays the bills, but one that you can be proud of, and one that you look forward to getting to every morning.

The Equipment

You're out of prison, and you're looking for a job. Where do you begin?

The first step is recognizing that you need the proper equipment to conduct your job search. A wise carpenter does not begin a job without having a hammer, a saw, and the other tools needed to complete his task from beginning to end. As a job seeker, what tools will you need? Here is a good list.

> **Resume**

A resume is a brief summary and listing of your skills, experience, and qualifications. Resumes are often required by employers who are hiring for positions that need some special skills or knowledge. If you are applying for positions for which no experience is necessary, you probably can get away without a resume. But to maximize your job search, you should either prepare a resume or have one prepared.

Resumes should never exceed two pages. Keep in mind that you may be submitting your resume to an employer who may have hundreds of resumes to flip through. If yours is exceedingly long, it may wind up in the trash bin without being looked at. So, respect the employer's time and make your resume long enough to adequately detail what you have to offer, but short enough for the employer to read quickly.

The resume is not your life story. There is no need to put hobbies, pets, membership organizations, number of children you have, and other family details on a resume unless they are relevant to the job you are seeking. Following is the format of a typical resume:

HEADING

Should include your full name, your mailing address, a reliable telephone number, and an e-mail address if your have one. If, during your job search, you are expecting to move to another address, list that one as well. If you are going to be moving around a bit, it may be best to spend a few bucks to get a PO Box.

OBJECTIVE STATEMENT

The objective is a brief statement of the type of position you are seeking, in what field or industry, and what you bring to that position.

This statement is very important and should be written with care. It serves as an introduction to what follows and lets the employer know whether this resume will fit with the position she has available. Since this statement is so important, it is not uncommon for a job seeker to have several resumes, with a different objective on each, tailored to the job which he is seeking. The objective should never be written too general. For example, consider this objective:

Seeking a career where I can use my many skills to enhance business operations.

Sounds good, doesn't it? But what does it say? It does not tell the employer what career you are interested in, or what skills you have, or how they will strengthen his business. The employer has to read the rest of your resume to figure that out. And chances are he will not bother.

An objective such as the one listed above tells the employer, "I do not care what job I get. I just want a job." That is the last thing you want to tell an employer.

Let's take another example. Let's say you are applying for a position as a carpenter for a construction company. Read the following objective:

Seeking a position in carpentry that will utilize my ten years of experience and skills to enhance company operations.

Okay, now we're talking. The objective lists the position wanted (carpentry), mentions the amount of experience (ten years), and mentions that those skills will enhance company operations, which speaks to the employer's sense of WIIFM (What's In It For Me). Therefore, if the employer is looking for a skilled carpenter, you have her attention.

It is important to sell yourself in the objective. You have only a few words to effectively summarize your entire resume and get the employer to read further.

SKILLS AND KNOWLEDGE

This section should be presented next, particularly if you have little job experience and little formal education. Here you should list in detail the skills and abilities that you bring to the position. The skills and abilities you list should be tailored to your objective. If your objective is to become a carpenter, it does not matter if you can cook a mean omelet. Leave off any skills not relevant to the objective.

Present your skills in a manner that is enticing to the employer. Don't just simply say, "I know how to use carpentry tools." (So do I, but that does not necessarily make me qualified for the position). List your skills, the number of years you have used those skills, and the settings in which you have used those skills. Which of the following do you think is better?

- *Knowledgeable about carpentry tools*
- *Two years' experience using a wide variety of carpentry tools to help build and repair homes and churches.*

The second statement gives more detail, including the number of years of experience and the setting in which the skill was used.

QUALIFICATIONS

Many jobs, in addition to the skills and knowledge needed to perform the task effectively, require attention to detail, patience, the ability to work with supervision, a pleasant speaking voice, etc. These characteristics are associated with an individual's personality rather than formal training and education. Here, it is helpful to assess yourself and list the personal traits you have that are relevant to and can help qualify you for the position. For instance, if you are applying to be a secretary or administrative assistant and have a pleasant speaking voice, that may help further qualify you for the position, since secretary and AA positions involve frequent answering of telephones. Or, if you are applying for a job in customer service, being a patient person will certainly help you sell yourself to an employer.

EMPLOYMENT

Depending on whom you talk to, some people would recommend listing this section first in your resume. Others would disagree, saying it should be last. I say it depends on how strong a job history you have. If you have never held a job, either inside or outside prison, whether paid or volunteer, I would just omit this section entirely. However, if you have had at least one job, list it under this section.

List job titles, dates of employment, the organization worked for, location (city, state) of the organization, and a description of your duties and how they benefited the employer. List the most recent job first. List both paid and volunteer positions. In listing jobs, you may have some jobs that are irrelevant to the objective or your skills presented. However, if these jobs fill significant gaps in your resume, include them for the sake of displaying that you have held some jobs, even if they are not relevant to your current objective.

EDUCATION

If you have only a General Equivalency Diploma (GED) or a high school diploma, list it here. If you have completed any education beyond high school, leave off the diploma or GED (since it is likely you have one if you have postsecondary educational experience) and list either the school or the degree, according to the following criteria:

- *If degree, list the degree title first and then the graduation date.*
  If school, list the school first and then the location.
  Include the name of the degree/major, school, location, and minor or certificate
  Include GPA - cumulative; may add major or upper division GPA to better showcase performance.
  Highlight education that is relevant to the position; leave out info common to all people in your field.
- *Include relevant courses that showcase your skills, knowledge, and talents that you are marketing to the employer.*

ACTIVITIES/AFFILIATIONS/INTERESTS

If they are relevant to your objective, list any extra activities, affiliations, memberships, or interests that you are involved in outside of work. These show the employer that you are interested in your objective even if you are not doing it on a professional level.

Style of Resume

Type Size
Your resume should be typed in a font that is easy to read and understand. Your resume should not be typed in anything smaller than **10-point type**, or anything larger than **14-point type.** Type size should be uniform throughout the resume.

Type Style
Type your resume in a **Times New Roman type** or **Helvetica type**, which are the type styles most commonly used by businesses.

Other Resume Style Points
- Have your resume checked for grammatical or spelling errors.
- Do not include photographs, graphics, or clip art with your resume.
- Put your name and the section headings of the resume in **bold-faced type**.
- Print your resume on good-quality, 24 lb, 8-1/2" x 11" white or off-white paper with black ink. Do not use bright or pastel colors.
- If your resume exceeds one page, use two separate pieces of paper. Do not print on the front and back of one sheet of paper.
- At the top of the second page of your resume, put your full name on the left-hand side, the word "Resume" in the center, and "Page No. 2" on the right-hand side.
- Leave out the "References Available upon Request" section that appears in many resumes. Most employers understand this to be true, and will ask for references if they need them.
- Place bullets in front of each listing, so the reader can separate the various points and listings in the resume. The listing you are reading now has bullets at the beginning of each paragraph.

Now, make several copies of your resumes (make sure they are on the same quality paper as the original resume), fold them in half, tuck them into a Day Planner (see below) with your cover letter (next section) and other documents, and carry them with you wherever you go until you find a job. Always have a resume ready to put into the hands of anyone who either is hiring or knows someone who is.

➤ **Cover Letter**

If you are sending out a resume via mail or to a person to whom you have not been introduced, you should always include a cover letter with your resume. A cover letter should be no more than one to two pages and serves the following purposes:

1) Makes sure that your resume goes to the right person or department.
2) States your objective. Rather that having your objective on the resume, it is best to have it in your cover letter, so you can tailor it to the specific company.
3) Highlights your skills and abilities as presented on the resume. Included in the cover letter should be a short narrative on your skills, abilities, training, education, and achievements, and why they would be a good fit for the company. If you are applying for a position that involves good speaking, writing, or communications skills, employers will be paying particular attention to how you construct your cover letter.
4) Why you want the job, and why you want to work for *that* particular company. Truth be told, you will probably work for anyone who offers you a job—you could probably care less about the company and its history. However, you should take the extra time and energy and find out a few details about the company, so you can explain in your cover letter how you can help that company fulfill its mission.
5) States that you are interested in the job and are interested in and available for an interview.

Since cover letters should be targeted to individuals and companies, you will want to have access to a computer with a printer so you can type your cover letters as you are informed of potential job openings. If you do not have a computer of your own, find a relative or friend who can let you use theirs, or find a library in your community that has computers available for public access. In addition, many city and state governments and community agencies have job search centers where you can get access to a computer.

Figure 1 below displays an example of the structure of a cover letter. This example can be adapted according to your needs.

Your name
Address
Phone
Email

Date

Contact Person's Name
Contact Person's Position
Company Name
Company Address (Do not forget this.)

Re: Name of position   or   Application for...

Dear Ms Jones (Avoid Dear Sir/Madam)

First paragraph
I would like to apply for the above position advertised in .... on........(date) and **why you want that job** (i.e. why that industry and why that company, make sure this highlights how you will meet their needs, not exclusively your own.)

Second / Third paragraph
Outline the skills (technical and social), experience, training and achievements that are relevant to the selection criteria or the job description. These skills may have been gained through your education/course, your work experience and your extra curricula activities.

Fourth paragraph
Tell them why you are the best fit for the company and how your skills will meet their needs. (Tip: you could summarize the three best things about you that make you most competitive for the job and how these things will allow you to make an impact/get results in the role.)

Closing
Thank them for considering your application. Tell them that you have attached a copy of your resume, and let them know when you would be available for an interview. Provide your contact details (Phone / Fax / Email)

Yours sincerely   *ask for the interview.*

Your signature

Print name

➤ **Clothing for Job Applications and Job Interviews (Comfortable Shoes)**

The clothing to wear during your job search and on interviews is very important. Your clothing must combine comfort with a neat, business or business casual look. As an ex-offender, particularly if you are fresh out of prison, you may not have a closet full of clothing from which to choose. But perhaps a relative or a friend or a community agency can help you with getting clothes that are suitable for the job search. Remember, image is very important in the job search. A slovenly or unkempt image is likely to translate into a slovenly and unkempt work ethic. That is the LAST impression you want to leave on employers.

Common wisdom says you must wear neat clothing to job interviews. However, I would recommend wearing it even when you are on the streets looking for employment or are applying for a position. I say this for several reasons:

1) You might be interviewed on the spot based on your application, and you want to look good.
2) The person taking your application may also be the person who will hire you, so you want to leave a good impression the first time.
3) You never have to delay a meeting, interview, or contact, because you are dressed inappropriately.

I am not suggesting that you have to wear a suit while looking for a job. However, clean, comfortable business or business casual clothing is essential. Here is a suggested "uniform" for the job seeker:

1) Hard- or soft-soled dress shoes.
2) Plain dark socks (no white socks, sweat socks, or socks with loud patterns).
3) Dark dress pants or khakis.
4) A leather or leather-like belt to match the shoes.
5) A buttoned-up, white or light-colored dress shirt or casual dress shirt. No polo shirts, T-shirts, jerseys, sweaters, or shirts with loud, bright colors.
6) A dark matching tie (optional for many blue-collar jobs).
7) A black or matching blazer (optional for many blue-collar jobs).

Yeah, I know. The outfit sounds boring and will not win you any fashion contests. However, the intent here is to blend into the business environment and avoid giving the employer a reason to pay particular attention to your clothes. If the employer barely notices what you are wearing, then you are right on the money in terms of your dress. But if you show up at a job interview looking like a rapper or a rock star, you can probably kiss that job good-bye, unless you are interviewing to be a musician. So, look your best, even if you are interviewing to be a trash collector.

➤ **Address of a Good Library**

Never underestimate the value of a good library. Libraries have a wealth of job search tools you can use, including computers to connect to the Internet and type resumes and cover letters, various newspapers that post help-wanted ads, access to telephone and business directories, etc. Some libraries offer job search seminars and other valuable resources for job seekers, and others post want ads from companies looking to hire. Each library varies in the type of information it has. Check with your local library, and let them know you are looking for employment.

> ### ➢ A Reliable Vehicle or Transportation Money

Whether you live in the town or country, you will need to be able to get around, sometimes on a moment's notice. If you can get access to a reliable vehicle (preferably your own), that would be the ideal tool (and may increase your qualifications for jobs, since some jobs require you to have a car or other reliable transportation). If you cannot get a car of your own or borrow one, then maybe a relative or friend can help by offering to take you to job sites or job interviews.

If you cannot get a reliable vehicle and you live in a major city with public transportation, then you may not need a car. Most buses, trains, and subways run during business hours, when most people are likely to be working. Borrow some money from friends or relatives for transportation money to get around, or contact a community agency in your area that helps people find jobs. They may have transportation subsidies to help you with the costs of public transportation.

This is a very important area. The last thing you want is to have an interview scheduled, and then not have the means to get there. Try to plan and secure your transportation needs days ahead.

> ### ➢ Telephone Directory

Ah, yes, that thick yellow book the local telephone companies publish. This will be your secret weapon, and you will do well to get your hands on your own copy before you begin your job search. Once you get one, you will have in your hands the names, telephone numbers, and addresses of almost every legitimate employer in town.

> ### ➢ Day Planner

Unless you are in business, you probably have no idea what a Day Planner is. A Day Planner is the term for a product that incorporates a calendar, a telephone book, a notepad, and a few other nifty items to help you "plan your day." They are usually available with a plastic or leather case approx. 5-1/2" x 8-1/2" that you can use to hold documents such as your resume or your birth certificate. If someone you know wants suggestions for something to get you for Christmas, and a new car is a bit too expensive for them, this would be a great suggestion. You can use this to carry all your job-related documents, and the calendar and telephone book will come in handy.

> ### ➢ Documents to Establish Employment Eligibility

By federal law, employers must verify that you are eligible to work in the United States before they can allow you to report to work. In the appendix of this book is a copy of an I-9 form issued by the US Immigration and Naturalization Service. On page three of the form is a list of documents that you must present to the employer before beginning work. Many employers, to avoid wasting time on hiring non-eligible individuals, may ask you to verify your employment eligibility at the time of application or during the interview. Be ready. Get the required documents listed on page three of the I-9 form and have them always handy.

> **Police Clearance**

Employers that are hiring for security-sensitive positions may conduct a thorough background check on their own to verify your job history, criminal history, credit record, and other details. However, some employers, not wanting to go through the time and expense of such a check, may require only that you present a clean police record for the past seven to ten years. Therefore, you should go to the local police department of every town in which you have lived in the past ten years and request a clearance report. If they have no record, request a signed letter on police department letterhead indicating that they have no record of any offenses. You will need to present some form of ID, and you may need to pay a small fee to obtain the report.

When you receive your police clearance, check it carefully. Verify the accuracy of any offenses listed on the report. If there is any inaccurate information listed, you should get this information removed, because it could affect your employment choices. Even if the information is accurate, you may be able to get the information sealed, which would prevent it from showing up on the clearance. Check with a legal service in your jurisdiction for information on how to do this.

> **Names, Addresses, and Telephone Numbers of at least Four References**

As a means of verifying your employability, employers may request the names, addresses, and telephone numbers of up to four people who know you well and can vouch for you.

Here is where many job seekers make mistakes. Employers will not know you from Adam, so they will want to hear that other people besides you recommend you. That goes a long way in helping you to get the job, and may even be the deciding factor in whether you are hired. Most employers check references only when they are seriously considering hiring you, so you need to make sure that your list of references is in good shape.

Whom should you list as a reference? If you have job experience, list people who have worked with you and can recommend you highly. Co-workers, supervisors, and managers are good references. Contact them and ask them for permission to be included in your reference list and tell them that potential employers may call them. Get their names, addresses, telephone numbers, and dates and times when they can be contacted. Put all of this information, along with the reference's relationship to you, on a piece of paper similar to your resume, and make several copies of it. If an employer asks you for reference information, give it to them. However, protect your references' privacy. Never give reference information to anyone other than someone who can hire you, and never give it unless requested.

Now, given that you may have been in prison the past ten years, you may not have many professional references. Many of the companies where you worked may no longer be in existence, and the co-workers with whom you worked may not be able to be found. In this case, it is permissible to use personal references, i.e., the names of professional people in the community who know you well and are willing to say nice things about you to help you get a job. However, you should choose these people carefully. Mothers, fathers, relatives, girlfriends, boyfriends, and spouses may say fantastic things about you, but they do not make good references. Neither will your friend from down the street. The employer wants to hear from people who have a professional relationship with you and are not related to you. Good references may include your pastor or other minister or community leader, politicians, teachers, lawyers, executives, social workers or case managers, or doctors. If the employer's policies permit, maybe you can get your supervisory officer or other criminal justice professional to serve as a reference.

➢ **Details of Past Employers**

Your resume will contain summary information on your past employers and work experience. However, when you fill out an application, you will be required to provide more details about each of your employers. Therefore, you will want to research the following information about each of your past employers, have the information typed on paper, put the info in your Day Planner, and have the information handy for completing applications:

- Name of Company
- Current Address of Company (not the address when you worked there)
- Name of Immediate Supervisor
- Current Telephone Number of Immediate Supervisor, if available
- Job Title
- Job Location (if different from company address)
- Job Duties
- Dates of Employment
- Reason for leaving employment (reduction-in-force, left for another position, terminated, career advancement, etc. Never say anything critical of your former employer)
- Starting Salary
- Ending salary
- Explanation for gaps in your employment history exceeding 90 days

As well as your work history, there are other items you will want to record and keep for job applications. See Appendix II, *Information You Should Collect For Your Job Search.*

➢ **Documents Showing Salary History**

This is a tricky one. Sometimes employers will ask you for your salary history, so they can determine whether you will be too expensive for them to consider you. Even though this information is asked many times on the application, you may be asked to provide this information when submitting a resume. Keep a list of past employers and the amounts they paid you handy, but do not give it to an employer unless she asks.

> ## Addresses of All Residences in the Past Ten Years (Other than Prison)
To conduct background checks, many employers ask you about past residences on their job applications. Make sure you have these addresses jotted down on a piece of paper and placed inside your Day Planner so you can provide the information.

> ## A Good Watch
You cannot be on time for interviews and appointments if you do not know what time it is. Buy or borrow a good watch. 'Nuff said.

> ## Cell Phone (If Affordable)
If you can afford a cell phone, get one. You can put the cell phone number on resumes and applications, and, if employers are interested in speaking with you further, they can reach you wherever you are. If you cannot afford a cell phone, then make sure the telephone number you give to employers to contact you is reliable, and the people answering are responsible in taking messages and relaying them to you. Nothing can derail your job search more than a telephone number that is always busy, or where messages are not given to you.

> ## Letter of Federal Bonding
The federal government and some state governments have fidelity bonding available for ex-offenders. Fidelity bonding is insurance made available to the ex-offender and covers the employer in case of theft or dishonesty by the ex-offender. This bonding program exists because of the reluctance of commercial bonding programs to provide bonding to ex-offenders based on their backgrounds.

You can obtain more information on the Federal Bonding program by writing or calling your state employment agency, or by writing the Federal Bonding Program, 1725 DeSales Street NW, Suite 900, Washington, DC 20036. Their telephone number is 202-293-5566 or 800-233-2258. The web site is www.bonds4jobs.com.

> ## Information about the Work Opportunity Tax Credit Act
Employers who hire people in certain groups, including low-income ex-offenders, can claim a tax credit on their federal tax returns. This credit, 35% of the first $6,000 of wages paid to an eligible employee, is an added incentive for employers to hire ex-offenders. You can obtain the required paperwork for applying for the tax credit as well as more information by calling the WOTC Program at 303-620-4224. Having this information with you, particularly during interviews, may provide an added incentive for for-profit employers to hire you.

What Is the Number One Thing Employers Are Looking For?

ANSWER: A Good Attitude!

Many employers make the mistake of hiring people with good skills but bad attitudes. They complain about everything. They use bad language. They feel the world owes them something, so they do not want to work. They come to work inappropriately dressed. They are ready to protest the moment the boss gives them something to do that is not in their job description. An employee with a bad attitude can affect the work environment, delay or hinder production, and even embarrass the company. Therefore, it does not matter if you are the best bricklayer in town. If you come to work late simply because you have ten kids and you feel it is your right, or if you use bad language on the job because "everybody's using bad language these days," or if you complain at every little thing the boss asks you to do, then you become a liability to the company. In fact, many employees are fired simply because of their bad attitudes.

It does not matter how good your skills are. Skills can be taught, and many employers are willing to do so. A good attitude cannot, and I do not know of a single employer who wants to take the time and make the effort to try. Therefore, it helps to reflect a good attitude during the job search and throughout any resulting employment.

The Christian writer Charles Swindoll once said:
The longer I live, the more I realize the impact of attitude on life. Attitude to me is more important than facts. It is more important than the past, than education, than money, than circumstances, than failures, than success, than what other people think or say or do. It is more important than appearance, gift, or skill. It will make or break a company...a church...a home. The remarkable thing is we have a choice every day regarding the attitude we will embrace for that day. We cannot change our past...we cannot change the fact that people will act in a certain way. We cannot change the inevitable. The only thing we can do is play on the string we have, and that is our attitude. I am convinced that life is 10 percent what happens to me and 90 percent how I react to it. And so it is with you... we are in charge of our attitudes.

You would do well to adopt that approach in your job search. Take charge of your attitude. A good attitude reflected in your job search is very likely to enhance your chances of finding a job, even if your skills and experience are nothing to write home about.

Reflections of a bad attitude
1) Wearing attire, hairstyles, or jewelry that is inappropriate to the job. Inquire of your employer what would be proper apparel and hairstyle to wear to the job, and have a willingness to abide, within reason, by the employer's mandate.
2) Making excuses for not getting to work on time. Come to work on time.
3) Unwillingness to work overtime. Employers love employees who are willing to put in extra time to get their jobs done.
4) Treating the boss and other employees with disrespect. It does not matter how they treat you. Do not let them draw you down to their level. Always deal respectfully and professionally with your boss and fellow employees. Avoid arguments, if possible. If you find yourself in a conflict, be willing to listen to the other view and work on a solution.
5) Use of bad language.
6) Lack of a smile.
7) Not keeping oneself busy, even if you have completed all of your assignments.
8) Not taking on assignments cheerfully, and completing them promptly.
9) Bad-mouthing the company, other employees or supervisors.
10) Being mean and unaccommodating.
11) Frequent grumbling and complaining.
12) Unwillingness to learn.

Do yourself a favor. Present yourself as an asset to any company. Employers are looking for people with positive attitudes. Your attitude determines your altitude.

Where Do I Start Looking?

If you have read and studied this far in the book and are willing to abide by all the principles discussed here, you will have an advantage over many job seekers in that you will be well prepared. Having been properly equipped and having a clear idea of the direction you will go on your job search, now you are ready to wade into the rough waters of the American job market.

The notion there are no jobs out there is false. In fact, there are plenty of jobs out there. The problem is there are too many people after them. So, finding a job is a competition that you must win. That is why they call it the job *market*. A market is a place where various products or services are sold. You are now part of the job market, and there are employers out there looking for you. The process of linking the employer and the job seeker is a process we will call *marketing*.

Let's look at Webster's definition of the term "marketing":

The commercial functions involved in transferring goods from producer to consumer. In the job market, you are the producer, the employer is the consumer. In any good marketing strategy, it is the producer's responsibility to get his product into the hands of the consumer, not the other way around. Therefore, it is not the employer's responsibility to find you. You have to find him.

One of the marketer's most effective tools is advertising. This is her method of letting the public know about her product or service in a way that makes the product attractive. The more people see her ads, the more likely her product will sell. Therefore, an effective marketer will try to expose her product or service to as many people as possible who are likely to need her product or service.

So, for you to find a job, you have to find those people who are in the position to hire you. You also have to find those people who *know* people who can hire you. To succeed, you must do this relentlessly. Every chance you get, let somebody know you are looking for work. And never give up.

Here are some ideas as to where you can begin your job search. To be successful, you should employ not just one or two, but *all* the following resources in your search.

Grocery store/community center bulletin boards

Community places such as grocery stores, libraries, community centers, and recreation centers are likely to have bulletin boards where job opportunities are posted. Make your rounds of these places and jot down any job-related leads.

Friends, relatives

This is the number one resource where most people find jobs. Employers love to hire people whom they know, or are referred by other employees. Let all of your friends and relatives know you are looking for employment and ask them to be on the lookout and to provide you with any job leads. Take the initiative and follow up on them.

Internet

The Internet remains one of the largest sources of information for job seekers. Many companies post job openings on their web sites, and others post jobs in other top job-related web sites such as monster.com and hotjobs.com. Go online to an internet search engine such as Yahoo or Google (get a friend or relative knowledgeable in computers to help you with this, if needed), and type in the phrase *jobs online*. Then, carefully check out every web site listed for possible job leads.

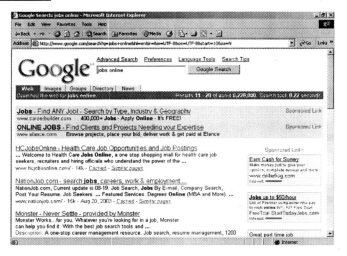

You can also use search engines to seek out companies that may be hiring in your chosen career. See *Telephone Directories* below.

Newspapers

We know about the standard classified ads that appear in the want ads section of every city newspaper. This classic method of finding a large listing of employers looking for employees has fallen victim to the computer age, but remains a viable source of information about jobs.

Telephone Directories

The thick yellow book sitting under your mom's coffee table is probably the most effective, yet most underutilized, tool available to job seekers. If you have targeted your job search to one or more specific careers, you can use the telephone directories to look up all those companies that are likely to employ people in your chosen career. For instance, if you are looking for cleaning work, you might look under the section in the directory called "Janitorial Companies," call all the companies listed, and ask if they have any jobs available.

The advantage of this is you are likely to find companies that are hiring that may not have had the time or expense to post a classified ad, or you may find companies that post jobs only on their own job line or through their personnel office. When making cold calls to these companies, always be friendly (even if the person who answers the phone is not so friendly) and inquire about any available job openings. If the company has no job openings available, then ask for permission to send them a cover letter and resume in case jobs become available in the future. Get a mailing address and a contact name, if possible, and quickly mail the cover letter and resume. Then move on to the next company.

If the company has openings, you may be rerouted to the personnel office, or the job hotline, or the person named Jack who sits in the front office and does all the hiring. If the company offers to send you a listing of job openings in the mail, and the company is not far away, politely inquire if you can pick it up instead. That way, you know you'll get it, rather than having to wait for a secretary to get around to mailing out your package. However, do not press the issue if the company would prefer to mail it.

Personal visits

Many companies prefer to advertise their vacancies by posting "help wanted" signs in their front lobby, or posting signs outside, or even on their vehicles traveling around town. Keep your eye out for such opportunities and pursue them. Even as you go about your daily business, you may discover companies that may have jobs of interest to you. Take the time, stop in, and inquire about any job openings.

Training programs and apprenticeships

If you are looking for a job and have to find one right away, a training or apprenticeship program may not seem like a good option, since they often involved a significant investment of time. Let me give you some reasons why you should reconsider.

First, a training or apprenticeship *may be the best way* for an unskilled ex-offender to gain skills that will be valuable in the workforce. An apprenticeship is a special training program in which the student gets on-the-job training combined with practical classroom instruction. Many apprenticeship programs offer pay to the student, which often increases as the student moves closer toward the end of his training. Apprenticeship programs are not only the domain of blue-collar workers, as secretaries and even IT professionals often get their jobs through apprenticeships.

Should you decide to take part in an apprenticeship or training program, you should participate in one that has been certified by your state training, apprenticeship, or employment agency. This brings me to the next section.

Federal and state government employment services

In almost every state and city, a government agency helps the disadvantaged connect with employment. Check the telephone directory or call directory information to find the agency closest to you. Then call them, make an appointment, and go to see what they have to offer. Many can get you access to training and apprenticeship programs, on-the-job training, computers to aid in your job search, and employment listings, among other things.

The federal government also has many resources to aid you in your job search. To best access these resources, find a computer, get online, and access the following web sites:

US Department of Labor main web page   *www.dol.gov*
Main web page for the DOL, the federal government's workforce development agency.

US Department of Labor Employment and Training Administration
www.doleta.gov

America's Job Bank   *www.ajb.org*
America's Job Bank is the biggest and busiest job market in cyberspace. Job seekers can post their resume where thousands of employers search every day, search for job openings automatically, and find their dream job fast. Employers can post job listings on the nation's largest online labor exchange, create customized job orders, and search resumes automatically to find the right people fast.[1]

America's Career InfoNet   *www.acinet.org*
America's Career InfoNet (ACINet) helps people make better, more informed career decisions. America's Career InfoNet is ideal for job seekers, employers, human resource specialists, and workforce development specialists.[2]

America's Service Locator   *www.servicelocator.org*
America's Service Locator and the Toll-Free Help Line (1-877-US-2JOBS) is a partnership between the US Department of Labor, state governments, and local agencies to provide a comprehensive database of service providers accessible via phone or the Internet to the public. Use of the database is free of charge and directs customers to a range of services available in their area: unemployment benefits, job training, youth programs, seminars, education opportunities, disabled or older worker programs, and much, much more.[3]

---

[1] Reprinted from web site
[2] Reprinted from web site
[3] Reprinted from web site

Office of Personnel Management *www.usajobs.opm.gov*
The Office of Personnel Management regulates employment with the federal government. All federal government jobs must be listed with this office.

Private Employment Agencies

In addition to the services offered by the government, many private employment agencies also offer help to the job seeker, and may be able to do it without the bureaucracy of many government agencies. You can find these agencies by checking your telephone directory under employment agencies or by checking with your local government to see which agencies are licensed or certified.

Temporary Agencies

To a person looking for permanent, steady work, the idea of going to a temporary agency may seem unappealing. Temporary agencies usually offer short-term jobs, usually less than one year. However, do not discount them. Even a short-term job is better than no job. Occasionally, a short-term job has led to permanent employment. In addition, having a job, even a temporary one, can make it easier to find employment because the employer is more likely to hire you if you are already employed. Why is this? The same reason why you probably will not try out a restaurant if it is starkly empty during a workweek lunch hour. To an employer, if no one is taking advantage of your services, there is a good chance that no one wants to. Having a job makes you more employable in the eyes of the employer.

Temporary agencies often maintain a pool of trained, screened employees, which they then send to companies in need of instant, qualified personnel. Sometimes, jobs last for only a week. In other cases, jobs can last for a year or more. Many temporary worker agencies specialize in certain types of jobs, such as secretarial or administrative, or janitorial, or food service. You will return to your ol' standby, the telephone directory. Check out listings under Temp Agency, temporary agencies, or similar listings. Check out the temporary agency to make sure they have the kinds of jobs that suit you.

The Interview and Follow-Up

It is the moment in every job search that causes the most excitement and anticipation, yet also the most anxiety. It is a crucial moment that every job seeker wants to achieve short of actually being hired. It is the moment that can determine whether your job search ends soon, or continues for a little while longer.

It is the moment when the employer calls you in for an interview.

Usually when this happens, the employer has reviewed your application, resume, and other paperwork you have submitted, and likes you enough that he or she wants to talk to you further. In job talk, this is called "getting your foot in the door."

How the interview occurs varies from job to job. In some situations, you may fill out an application and then go immediately to an interview. In others, you present the application and other paperwork in advance, and then you go home and hope and pray the employer calls you.

Interviews are for the employer to ask you questions to decide if he wants to hire you. But they are also for you to ask questions to decide if you want to work for him.

The key is to always be prepared for an interview, because you never know what interview scenario you will be up against. Never take on the attitude that "I will get ready for an interview when they call me for one."

As an ex-offender, preparation for an interview takes on extra significance. Ex-offenders who go to job interviews are likely to have to answer questions about their criminal history, their imprisonment, and their resulting rehabilitation. If you have applied for a job, and have made no attempt to hide that you are an ex-offender, a call for an interview usually indicates the employer is willing to hire you despite your criminal record. After all, if hiring ex-offenders were a problem with the employer, he wouldn't have called you in for the interview. So, you can assume that you have an employer who is receptive to you, despite your record.

If you have tried to hide your prison record, then the employer's interview request may be to find out, among other things, why there was a gap in your job history, or why you haven't had a job for several years, or why your last job is in a different state from your residence.

Whatever the scenario, the interview is your time to shine. You will have fifteen to thirty minutes to either convince the employer, or support his initial impression that hiring you is a good choice for his business.

I HAVE AN INTERVIEW: WHAT DO I DO?

If you are called in for an interview, follow the suggestions listed in the chapter "The Equipment" regarding clothing for job interviews.

If you are called in for an interview, carefully note the day, time, and place of the interview. Make sure the address is correct. Take down a telephone number where you can reach the interviewer in case there is a problem.

Then, immediately start adjusting your schedule.

Since getting an interview is a major milestone for a job seeker, you will want to make sure that the day and time of the interview is cleared. Do not schedule anything before the interview. (You do not want a commitment before the interview to run over schedule and interfere with your timely arrival at the interview.) Nor should you schedule anything after the interview that may cause you to have to leave the interview before it is over. Interviews can be anywhere from ten to fifteen minutes to three hours and over (depending on the job, the number of interviewers, and whether you have to take an exam or perform other tasks). Make sure you have enough time so you do not have to rush yourself and create further anxiety.

Then arrange transportation. If you are driving your own car, or having a friend drive you to the interview, or are borrowing a friend's car, make sure you have a backup plan. Because sometimes cars break down, and friends don't arrive when they say they will. Be prepared in case something unexpected happens. For instance, if you are driving your own car, you may want to have some public transportation money and routes ready in case your car breaks down. If you are having a friend drive you, you may want to have another friend standing by, just in case.

Also, you will want to research the route to the interview site. You do not want to get lost. If you can, it would be helpful to simply drive to the interview site sometime before the day and time of the interview to familiarize yourself with the route.

Plan to arrive at the interview at least fifteen to thirty minutes before the interview time. One of the biggest mistakes you can make in time management is to plan to arrive exactly at your targeted time. Should something unexpected occur that causes you to be delayed, you will be late for the interview. So, if the interview starts at 11 a.m., plan to arrive between 10:30 and 10:45 a.m., to allow for delays such as traffic, getting lost, or any other unexpected instance.

On the day of the interview, avoid smoking or drinking. (These behaviors can create odors that are an immediate turn-off to an employer.) If the employer detects the odor of alcohol, he may think you are an alcoholic and will not hire you. If the employer smells cigarette smoke, he may not hire you because he knows you are going to spend at least an hour a day of productive work time taking cigarette breaks.

Make sure you are well-groomed and clean before the interview. Hair and nails should be clean and well-groomed. Wear deodorant, and avoid excessively strong cologne or perfume. Make sure you do not have bad breath. If you have a cold or other temporary sickness that causes you to sneeze, sniff, cough, or have red eyes, make sure you tell the employer of this upon the initial greeting, so the employer will not have reason to think that you are suffering from some other ailment.

Okay, so all of that stuff is easy. The hard part is walking into the interviewer's office and beginning the interview. This could be the time that literally changes your life. It is very important.

The first thing you do is to observe. If you have to wait before the interview starts, take this time to look around and make some observations. Note any plaques on the walls. Note the dress code of the employees. If the company has its brochures or other promotional documents on display, read them. Your goal here is to get a general idea of the company you are interviewing with, and may even result in a few questions for your interviewer.

When greeting the interviewer, smile, but do not appear excessively gleeful. If the interviewer extends a hand, give a firm handshake. Make eye contact during the entire interview, and do not fidget or engage in other nervous gestures, such as picking nails, doodling, wringing your hands, tapping your feet, etc. Do not smoke or eat during the interview. You may drink something if the interviewer offers it, but if it is not offered, do not partake.

Before the interview, sometimes interviewers will make small talk, such as asking or commenting about the weather, or about your trip to the office. Respond suitably with a few sentences, but do not talk too long or become too chatty. If you have any extra documentation to give to the interviewer, such as an updated resume, make sure that the interviewer gets it before the beginning of the interview so she has time to review it before the interview starts.

At this point, the interviewer may describe the job and give you more information about it than you previously had. Make sure you listen carefully and intently to anything the interviewer says. It is permissible to take a small notepad and pen into the interview and jot down important points or any questions that come to mind during the interview.

After all, there is a reason they call this a job interview. It is the employer's opportunity to pepper you with many questions so the employer can determine your fitness for employment. How you answer these questions can make a difference whether you are employed or not.

Richard Nelson Bolles, in his best-selling book *What Color is Your Parachute*, says that of all the many questions that are asked during a job interviewer, there are only five basic questions the employer wants to know:
- **Why are you here?**
- **What can you do for us?**
- **What kind of person are you?**
- **What distinguishes you from nineteen other people who can do the same tasks that you can?**
- **Can I afford you?**[4]

You would do well to have answers to these questions before you go to the job interview. The interviewer may phrase his questions differently, asking "Tell me about yourself" as a substitute for "What kind of person are you?"

Let's look at these questions in depth.

WHY ARE YOU HERE?

Do not misunderstand this question. The employer is not asking why you need a job. The employer wants to know two things: 1) why you are not currently employed, and if you are, why are you so dissatisfied with your current job that you are looking for a new one? 2) Of all the companies and jobs and businesses and professions, why did you darken *his* doorstep?

Being an ex-offender, the first part of this question can be scary and difficult to answer. If you are just getting out of jail or prison and are looking for a job, you may have to answer questions related to why you have a multi-year gap in your employment record. This will lead to discussions about your criminal record.

Some questions the employer asks about your criminal history may be illegal. We advise that you contact your state's labor agency and find out what the laws are in your state regarding questions that can be asked at job interviews regarding your criminal record. In some states, employers can ask about and consider convictions on your criminal record but not arrests that did not result in conviction. In some states, arrests not resulting in convictions may even be expunged from your record.

---

[4] Richard Nelson Bolles, *What Color is Your Parachute? A Practical Manual for Job Hunters and Career Changers,* 1998 ed. (City: Ten Speed Press, 1998) xx.

When confronted with the need to explain your criminal history in job interviews, we advise being honest about your history. You may be tempted to lie or disguise the fact that you have a criminal history, but if you are hired and your criminal history is discovered, you may get fired.

When answering questions about your history, do not dwell too heavily on the past. You may reveal the charge you were convicted of, and the details of your sentence, including any parole restrictions. But focus on your life now, especially what you have done to change your life and correct all the mistakes of the past. For instance, if your criminal record reveals alcohol or drug abuse, talk about your current rehabilitation efforts, especially any drug treatment you have had. It is important to participate in and speak of *continuing efforts* to get beyond your criminal past. Stress any mentoring programs or other special programs you are a part of.

The second part of the question deals with the reasons you picked the employer as a potential source of a job. If you followed the advice I gave earlier in this book about targeting your career, then you will have some idea of what job you are looking for. The way to answer this question is to explain what job you are looking for and why that company or that job fulfills your need for employment.

Many job search manuals recommend you do research on the company before going in for an interview. Such research will help you learn more about the company and whether they fit your personality and the career you are looking for.

WHAT CAN YOU DO FOR US?

Okay, so you thought you explained this in the seven-page application and the resume that you submitted to the employer. Isn't it obvious by now what you can do for the employer?

Actually the employer is not looking for you to simply recite your skills and abilities. He wants to know how you are going to use them to enhance his business. How are your skills and abilities going to affect his bottom line? Are you going to be a hindrance to his organization? For instance, if you are applying for a job in construction, how are your skills and abilities going to help him meet his deadlines and maintain compliance with regulations? If you are interested in employment as a hotel housekeeper, what benefits will the staff and guests see because of your service at his hotel? In other words, the employer wants to know how hiring you will make his business better than it was before he hired you.

1) As an ex-offender, be prepared to address the following concerns, whether the employer actually expresses them:
His fear that you will steal something from his company.
2) His fear that you will threaten or physically harm one of his employees.

3) His fear that you will be often absent from work because of drug abuse, re-arrests, parole officer meetings, laziness, and other reasons.

Again, stress that you have changed, and highlight current efforts to stay away from crime. Here also is an opportunity to talk about the Federal Bonding Program, which can potentially lessen or eliminate the employer's fear about theft in the workplace (see *Letter of Federal Bonding*, under the chapter "The Equipment").

WHAT KIND OF PERSON ARE YOU?

Earlier I spoke of the need to determine your personality. Go to that section, read it carefully, follow its advice, and then share all the positive aspects of your personality with your employer.

Sometimes the employer will throw at you a tricky question like:

1) Tell me something that if you could, you would change about your personality, or;
2) What is the worst thing about you?

Questions like this are designed to get you to say something negative about yourself. Sometimes the employer asks it to see what dirt he can dig up on you. Sometimes the employer asks it to see whether he has a truthful person. Therefore, if your response is "I do not have anything I would change about myself," the employer, knowing that no one is perfect, will write you off and move on.

The way to answer these types of questions is to share one or two things about yourself that you would change, but to make sure that the things do not affect your ability to do your job. Answers such as:

- "Sometimes I am a little too hard-working. I would like to relax more in my spare time."
- "I am a nice person and like to help, but sometimes people take advantage of that. I would like to become more aware of when people are simply trying to take advantage of me."

Responses like these reveal that you are human and have flaws, but none that are likely to affect your ability to do your job.

WHAT DISTINGUISHES YOU FROM NINETEEN OTHER PEOPLE WHO CAN DO THE SAME TASKS THAT YOU CAN?

This sounds like a trick question. After all, you do not know what the other nineteen people can or cannot do, so how can you distinguish yourself? Easy. By setting yourself at the top of the list. Stress that you will be at work on time, come to work every day, work hard, be respectful to supervisors and fellow staff, and have a positive attitude. These qualities are likely to make you the cream of the crop.

CAN I AFFORD YOU?

This, of course, has to do with the salary and fringe benefits you are asking for. You may be applying for a job where the salary the company is willing to pay has already been stated or will be stated, in which case you are off the hook. Otherwise, you will probably have to negotiate a compensation package with the employer.

If possible, avoid the discussion of salary and benefits until you have a written job offer. Then, ask the employer what he or she would be willing to pay.

But, in case the employer insists that you provide him with a salary requirement, you will need to research salary levels in your community for the job to which you are applying. (Check with your state labor department) This way, you will know what a suitable salary for the position is. Then, if you are asked what salary you would like, quote a salary about 10 to 15% higher than the levels in your research, but stress that it is open to negotiation and can be adjusted higher or lower.

The intent here is for you not to price yourself out of the market. You may be willing to accept any salary at this point, but a certain deal breaker is to quote a salary that is significantly higher than the employer's budget will allow.

QUESTIONS THE INTERVIEWER SHOULD NOT ASK YOU

Just because you are at a job interview does not mean the employer can ask you anything he wants. Because of anti-discrimination laws, employers are forbidden from asking you questions that probe race, national origin, sexual orientation, religion, age, marital status, family situation, or disabilities. There may be times in an interview when the employer may feel the need to get over-inquisitive and start to ask you questions along these lines. If you are desperate for employment, you may feel obligated to answer these questions, feeling that if you didn't, the employer wouldn't hire you. That is a legitimate concern. You could file a complaint against the interviewer, but who has time to do that if he is looking for a job?

If you are asked questions of this nature, you could do one of three things:
1) If you do not feel the questions are too probing, you may waive your rights and answer them to build a connection or rapport with the interviewer.
2) You could politely refuse to answer them; or
3) You could find out the real intent of the question and answer it that way. For instance, if the employer asks if you have a wife and kids (an illegal question), he may be trying to find out if you are too busy and wrapped up to perform the requirements of the job. You could simply answer, "Let me assure you there is nothing in my life, personally or otherwise, that will keep me from performing my

job." If the employer asks you, "What country are you from?" (an illegal question), he may be trying to determine if you can legally work in the United States. You may say, "I wasn't born in the United States, but I am a US citizen, and I am fully qualified to work in this country."

Not all questions of this type are illegal. In some situations, employers are allowed to discriminate. For instance, the federal anti-discrimination laws cover only certain employees (see "Appendix"). In addition, your race, national origin, or religion may be relevant in the job you are applying for, in which case the employer can ask you about it and even make job decisions based on it. For instance, if you were applying for an acting job playing the African-American Frederick Douglas on stage, the employer can hire only an African-American actor, since the actor's race lends to the realism of the play. Or, if you were interviewing to become a minister at a Christian church, questions about your religious beliefs are not only legal, they are in most cases expected.

NOW *YOUR* QUESTIONS

Once the interviewer has completed asking his questions, you should have an opportunity to ask the interviewer some questions. You should ask questions that are relevant to the job environment and performance and that are designed to find out if this is the place where you want to work. During the interview, the interviewer may have answered many of your questions about the job. Nonetheless, you should come prepared with a list of questions to ask.

The one thing you do not want to do is leave that interview without asking any questions. Asking questions shows interest in the company and the job. Even if during the interview, all of your questions have been answered, think of a couple more to ask, even if they only serve to clarify an answer that was previously given.

WHAT'S NEXT?

The employer has asked his questions, and you have asked yours. Now what? Will I be hired? Am I still being considered? Are you going to contact me, and if so, when? If the employer leaves these questions up in the air, you may want to inquire at the end of the interview as to whether you are still in the running, and if so, what next? Another interview? An exam? Or shall I just wait for a phone call?

These types of questions, asked politely and discreetly, show your interest in the job and keep you from having to wonder what's next in the process.

AFTER THE INTERVIEW

If you can get through the interview without breaking into a cold sweat, congratulations! Thank the interviewer, express your continued interest in the job, and leave at once. If you pass by a secretary or receptionist on the way out, thank him or her as well.

When you get home, you should do something that only a small percentage of job seekers do, something that will put you near the top of the ladder with some employers. Write a short thank you letter, once again expressing interest in the job. Drop it in the mail the next morning, without fail.

This single act of interest and professionalism can be, and often is, the single determinate factor in whether a job seeker is hired.

If the interviewer has told you when you could expect to hear from him, and he has not responded by the time, it is possible the interviewer was too busy and could not respond by his deadline date. Make a phone call and get an update as to when a decision will be made. Follow up with a short letter. If the second deadline dates passes, follow up with another letter.

After three post-interview contacts, if you have not heard anything, either yes or no, then you can end your contacts. If, after three post-interview contacts, you are still in the dark, it is likely that either the employer is not ready to hire yet, or he or she has no intention of hiring you, and simply has not told you. Either way, continue your job search and do not look back.

I'm Hired, I Think . . . .

One day, the phone rings at 8:30 a.m. Larry, an ex-offender with an armed robbery conviction who had gone on several interviews with companies in his city, answered the phone. It was a janitorial company that he had interviewed with just two days before. The employer said that they were pleased to offer him a job with their company cleaning office suites at a salary of $8.00 an hour. Larry, because he had been without a job for three months since leaving prison, was excited and immediately accepted. He asked that the company send him a written offer of employment so he could show his parole officer. The company agreed and mailed him the letter the following day. He was scheduled to arrive for his first day of work in two weeks.

Larry was ecstatic. He told his family, his parole officer, his friends, his neighbors, everyone. Finally his job search was over. He stopped his subscription to the local newspaper, and put away his resumes and other job search papers. In fact, he was called in for another interview, but he turned it down, since he got the offer with the janitorial company.

On his start day, Larry arrived for work that morning at the corporate office to complete some final paperwork, after which he understood he would be assigned to a team cleaning offices downtown. When he arrived at the corporate office, the receptionist showed him to a conference room, after which three men came in and sat at the table. They shut the conference room door and proceeded to tell Larry some news he had not been expecting.

The company's risk management department had heard about the job offer made to Larry. They ran a background check and discovered that Larry not only had an armed robbery conviction, but an armed robbery arrest for which he was not convicted. If they hired Larry, the company's professional liability insurance company would cancel their insurance policy. The company decided that hiring Larry was not worth the risk of losing their insurance.

The three men in suits told Larry that his written job offer was being rescinded, and that he would not be hired. Larry was angry, but being used to rejection, he took it in stride and left the offices.

What is the moral and prevailing lesson of this story?

Never, ever end your job search based on a job offer, or a job promise, or even if you *think* you are going to get the job.

In fact, wait until you have reported to the job and been working at least a week or two before you officially end your job search. That is also enough time for you to get to know your coworkers and the job environment and to find out if you really want to continue to work at this job.

Because Larry ended his job search the moment he found out about his job offer, he missed an opportunity for another interview and may have missed other opportunities of which he could have taken advantage. Had the job offer not been rescinded, he could have worked his job, and scheduled his job search activities around his work hours.

The only caution: only accept job offers you plan to accept. If you are working one job, and accept another offer while you are employed at the first job, you will probably have to quit the first job to take the second. Otherwise, the second employer may slap you with a lawsuit.

Appendixes

This part of the book contains forms and other important information relevant to the job search. Inside you will find:

Appendix I: **Employment Eligibility Verification Form (I-9)**
This form is used by employers to verify and certify an applicant's eligibility. Page three of the document is a list of documents that are acceptable to establish identity and employment eligibility.

Appendix II: **Information You Should Collect for Your Job Search**
List of items you should have on hand before beginning a serious job search.

Appendix III: **Summary of Federal Anti-discrimination Laws**

U.S. Department of Justice
Immigration and Naturalization Service

OMB No. 1115-0136

Employment Eligibility Verification

INSTRUCTIONS
PLEASE READ ALL INSTRUCTIONS CAREFULLY BEFORE COMPLETING THIS FORM.

Anti-Discrimination Notice. It is illegal to discriminate against any individual (other than an alien not authorized to work in the U.S.) in hiring, discharging, or recruiting or referring for a fee because of that individual's national origin or citizenship status. It is illegal to discriminate against work eligible individuals. Employers **CANNOT** specify which document(s) they will accept from an employee. The refusal to hire an individual because of a future expiration date may also constitute illegal discrimination.

Section 1 - Employee. All employees, citizens and noncitizens, hired after November 6, 1986, must complete Section 1 of this form at the time of hire, which is the actual beginning of employment. **The employer is responsible for ensuring that Section 1 is timely and properly completed.**

Preparer/Translator Certification. The Preparer/Translator Certification must be completed if Section 1 is prepared by a person other than the employee. A preparer/translator may be used only when the employee is unable to complete Section 1 on his/her own. However, the employee must still sign Section 1.

Section 2 - Employer. For the purpose of completing this form, the term "employer" includes those recruiters and referrers for a fee who are agricultural associations, agricultural employers or farm labor contractors.

Employers must complete Section 2 by examining evidence of identity and employment eligibility within three (3) business days of the date employment begins. If employees are authorized to work, but are unable to present the required document(s) within three business days, they must present a receipt for the application of the document(s) within three business days and the actual document(s) within ninety (90) days. However, if employers hire individuals for a duration of less than three business days, Section 2 must be completed at the time employment begins. **Employers must record: 1)** document title; **2)** issuing authority; **3)** document number, **4)** expiration date, if any; and **5)** the date employment begins. Employers must sign and date the certification. Employees must present original documents. Employers may, but are not required to, photocopy the document(s) presented. These photocopies may only be used for the verification process and must be retained with the I-9. **However, employers are still responsible for completing the I-9.**

Section 3 - Updating and Reverification. Employers must complete Section 3 when updating and/or reverifying the I-9. Employers must reverify employment eligibility of their employees on or before the expiration date recorded in Section 1. Employers **CANNOT** specify which document(s) they will accept from an employee.

- If an employee's name has changed at the time this form is being updated/ reverified, complete Block A.

- If an employee is rehired within three (3) years of the date this form was originally completed and the employee is still eligible to be employed on the same basis as previously indicated on this form (updating), complete Block B and the signature block.

- If an employee is rehired within three (3) years of the date this form was originally completed and the employee's work authorization has expired **or** if a current employee's work authorization is about to expire (reverification), complete Block B and:
  - examine any document that reflects that the employee is authorized to work in the U.S. (see List A or C).
  - record the document title, document number and expiration date (if any) in Block C, and complete the signature block.

Photocopying and Retaining Form I-9. A blank I-9 may be reproduced, provided both sides are copied. The Instructions must be available to all employees completing this form. Employers must retain completed I-9s for three (3) years after the date of hire or one (1) year after the date employment ends, whichever is later.

For more detailed information, you may refer to the INS Handbook for Employers, (Form M-274). You may obtain the handbook at your local INS office.

Privacy Act Notice. The authority for collecting this information is the Immigration Reform and Control Act of 1986, Pub. L. 99-603 (8 USC 1324a).

This information is for employers to verify the eligibility of individuals for employment to preclude the unlawful hiring, or recruiting or referring for a fee, of aliens who are not authorized to work in the United States.

This information will be used by employers as a record of their basis for determining eligibility of an employee to work in the United States. The form will be kept by the employer and made available for inspection by officials of the U.S. Immigration and Naturalization Service, the Department of Labor and the Office of Special Counsel for Immigration Related Unfair Employment Practices.

Submission of the information required in this form is voluntary. However, an individual may not begin employment unless this form is completed, since employers are subject to civil or criminal penalties if they do not comply with the Immigration Reform and Control Act of 1986.

Reporting Burden. We try to create forms and instructions that are accurate, can be easily understood and which impose the least possible burden on you to provide us with information. Often this is difficult because some immigration laws are very complex. Accordingly, the reporting burden for this collection of information is computed as follows: **1)** learning about this form, 5 minutes; **2)** completing the form, 5 minutes; and **3)** assembling and filing (recordkeeping) the form, 5 minutes, for an average of 15 minutes per response. If you have comments regarding the accuracy of this burden estimate, or suggestions for making this form simpler, you can write to the Immigration and Naturalization Service, HQPDI, 425 I Street, N.W., Room 4034, Washington, DC 20536. OMB No. 1115-0136.

EMPLOYERS MUST RETAIN COMPLETED FORM I-9
PLEASE DO NOT MAIL COMPLETED FORM I-9 TO INS

Form I-9 (Rev. 11-21-91)N

OMB No. 1115-0136

Employment Eligibility Verification

Please read instructions carefully before completing this form. The instructions must be available during completion of this form. **ANTI-DISCRIMINATION NOTICE:** It is illegal to discriminate against work eligible individuals. Employers CANNOT specify which document(s) they will accept from an employee. The refusal to hire an individual because of a future expiration date may also constitute illegal discrimination.

Section 1. Employee Information and Verification. To be completed and signed by employee at the time employment begins.

Print Name: Last	First	Middle Initial	Maiden Name

Address (Street Name and Number)	Apt. #	Date of Birth (month/day/year)

City	State	Zip Code	Social Security #

I am aware that federal law provides for imprisonment and/or fines for false statements or use of false documents in connection with the completion of this form.

I attest, under penalty of perjury, that I am (check one of the following):
☐ A citizen or national of the United States
☐ A Lawful Permanent Resident (Alien # A_____)
☐ An alien authorized to work until ___/___/___
(Alien # or Admission #) _____

Employee's Signature

Date (month/day/year)

Preparer and/or Translator Certification. *(To be completed and signed if Section 1 is prepared by a person other than the employee.) I attest, under penalty of perjury, that I have assisted in the completion of this form and that to the best of my knowledge the information is true and correct.*

Preparer's/Translator's Signature	Print Name

Address (Street Name and Number, City, State, Zip Code)	Date (month/day/year)

Section 2. Employer Review and Verification. To be completed and signed by employer. Examine one document from List A OR examine one document from List B and one from List C, as listed on the reverse of this form, and record the title, number and expiration date, if any, of the document(s)

List A	OR	List B	AND	List C

Document title: _____

Issuing authority: _____

Document #: _____

Expiration Date (if any): ___/___/___

Document #: _____

Expiration Date (if any): ___/___/___

List B: ___/___/___   List C: ___/___/___

CERTIFICATION - I attest, under penalty of perjury, that I have examined the document(s) presented by the above-named employee, that the above-listed document(s) appear to be genuine and to relate to the employee named, that the employee began employment on *(month/day/year)* ___/___/___ and that to the best of my knowledge the employee is eligible to work in the United States. (State employment agencies may omit the date the employee began employment.)

Signature of Employer or Authorized Representative	Print Name	Title

Business or Organization Name	Address (Street Name and Number, City, State, Zip Code)	Date (month/day/year)

Section 3. Updating and Reverification. To be completed and signed by employer.

A. New Name (if applicable)	B. Date of rehire (month/day/year) (if applicable)

C. If employee's previous grant of work authorization has expired, provide the information below for the document that establishes current employment eligibility.

Document Title: _____   Document #: _____   Expiration Date (if any): ___/___/___

I attest, under penalty of perjury, that to the best of my knowledge, this employee is eligible to work in the United States, and if the employee presented document(s), the document(s) I have examined appear to be genuine and to relate to the individual.

Signature of Employer or Authorized Representative	Date (month/day/year)

Form I-9 (Rev. 11-21-91)N Page 2

LISTS OF ACCEPTABLE DOCUMENTS

LIST A
Documents that Establish Both Identity and Employment Eligibility

1. U.S. Passport (unexpired or expired)

2. Certificate of U.S. Citizenship (INS Form N-560 or N-561)

3. Certificate of Naturalization (INS Form N-550 or N-570)

4. Unexpired foreign passport, with I-551 stamp or attached INS Form I-94 indicating unexpired employment authorization

5. Permanent Resident Card or Alien Registration Receipt Card with photograph (INS Form I-151 or I-551)

6. Unexpired Temporary Resident Card (INS Form I-688)

7. Unexpired Employment Authorization Card (INS Form I-688A)

8. Unexpired Reentry Permit (INS Form I-327)

9. Unexpired Refugee Travel Document (INS Form I-571)

10. Unexpired Employment Authorization Document issued by the INS which contains a photograph (INS Form I-688B)

OR

LIST B
Documents that Establish Identity

1. Driver's license or ID card issued by a state or outlying possession of the United States provided it contains a photograph or information such as name, date of birth, gender, height, eye color and address

2. ID card issued by federal, state or local government agencies or entities, provided it contains a photograph or information such as name, date of birth, gender, height, eye color and address

3. School ID card with a photograph

4. Voter's registration card

5. U.S. Military card or draft record

6. Military dependent's ID card

7. U.S. Coast Guard Merchant Mariner Card

8. Native American tribal document

9. Driver's license issued by a Canadian government authority

For persons under age 18 who are unable to present a document listed above:

10. School record or report card

11. Clinic, doctor or hospital record

12. Day-care or nursery school record

AND

LIST C
Documents that Establish Employment Eligibility

1. U.S. social security card issued by the Social Security Administration (other than a card stating it is not valid for employment)

2. Certification of Birth Abroad issued by the Department of State (Form FS-545 or Form DS-1350)

3. Original or certified copy of a birth certificate issued by a state, county, municipal authority or outlying possession of the United States bearing an official seal

4. Native American tribal document

5. U.S. Citizen ID Card (INS Form I-197)

6. ID Card for use of Resident Citizen in the United States (INS Form I-179)

7. Unexpired employment authorization document issued by the INS (other than those listed under List A)

Illustrations of many of these documents appear in Part 8 of the Handbook for Employers (M-274)

Form I-9 (Rev. 10/4/00)Y Page 3

APPENDIX II
INFORMATION YOU SHOULD COLLECT FOR YOUR JOB SEARCH

So that you may gather information, paperwork, etc. in advance, below is a list of the details employers typically want you to provide on job applications. It excludes the ordinary questions for which you do not need to prepare, such as your contact information.

- Social security number (SSN)
- Driver's license number and state of issue
- Whether or not you've been convicted of a crime by civil or military courts
  - Nature of the offense
  - Date of conviction
  - Location where convicted
  - Disposition (sentence, probation, etc.)
- Home addresses for the past ten years
- Date you're available for work
  - If you must give your current employer notice two weeks in advance, write *Two weeks notice*.
  - Otherwise, write the date on which you know for sure you can start work.
- Military service. Bring your discharge papers, just in case they ask to see them.
  - Entry and discharge dates
  - Type of discharge
  - Branch
  - Occupational specialization
  - Special training received and dates
  - Last rank
  - You might be asked if you are a veteran of a war, such as Vietnam. This is for affirmative action programs, not discrimination.
- Position desired, first and second choices.
- Geographic preference, first and second choices.
- Salary desired. If you want to temporarily sidestep the salary issue so you can negotiate, write *negotiable*, *open* or *competitive*.
- How you heard about the job
  - If an employee referred you, get the employee's work contact information in advance.
  - Then include it on the job application if required, so the employee receives incentives due.
- Education and training
  - Start and end dates
  - School names and addresses
  - Majors and minors
  - Degrees earned and dates
  - Grade point average
  - Rank in class

- Titles of Master's and Ph.D. Theses, and advisors' names
- Additional skills. Typically, you do not need to worry too much about these unless applicable for the job. For example, many workers type on computers these days, but words per minute (WPM) usually applies only to clerical jobs.
  - Typing WPM
  - Steno WPM
  - Professional licenses
  - Language fluency
  - Software knowledge
  - Equipment knowledge
  - Technical skills
- Professional organization memberships
  - Names of organizations
  - Dates of membership
  - Addresses and phone numbers
- Whether or not you are authorized to work in the country. If you have a work visa or were not a citizen at birth, be sure to bring relevant paperwork.
- Up to four references
  - Business and home addresses
  - Day and evening phone numbers
  - Occupations
  - Relationships to you
- Whether or not you've previously applied for work or worked at the same company. If so:
  - Dates of application or employment
  - Divisions, units, and departments for which you worked
  - Names of bosses
- Work history
  - Names of employers, including current employer
  - Mailing and street addresses (if different) and phone numbers. Provide this information for the offices where the Human Resources (HR) departments or your work records are located.
  - Start and end dates. Write present for the ending date at your current employer.
  - Reasons for leaving. Be careful with this one. Never criticize a former employer. Instead, write something generic like career advancement.
  - Last or beginning and ending salaries. If you want to temporarily sidestep salary issues or don't think it's any of their business, leave it blank or write *competitive*.
  - Bosses'' names, titles, and business contact information
  - Your job titles and the type of work you did
  - Reasons for gaps of 90 days or more in your work history, other than school

Reprinted from the web site of *The U.S. Equal Employment Opportunity Commission.*

Federal Laws Prohibiting Job Discrimination Questions And Answers

Federal Equal Employment Opportunity (EEO) Laws

I. What Are the Federal Laws Prohibiting Job Discrimination?

- Title VII of the Civil Rights Act of 1964 (Title VII), which prohibits employment discrimination based on race, color, religion, sex, or national origin;
- the Equal Pay Act of 1963 (EPA), which protects men and women who perform substantially equal work in the same establishment from sex-based wage discrimination;
- the Age Discrimination in Employment Act of 1967 (ADEA), which protects individuals who are 40 years of age or older;
- Title I and Title V of the Americans with Disabilities Act of 1990 (ADA), which prohibit employment discrimination against qualified individuals with disabilities in the private sector, and in state and local governments;
- Sections 501 and 505 of the Rehabilitation Act of 1973, which prohibit discrimination against qualified individuals with disabilities who work in the federal government; and
- the Civil Rights Act of 1991, which, among other things, provides monetary damages in cases of intentional employment discrimination.

The U.S. Equal Employment Opportunity Commission (EEOC) enforces all of these laws. EEOC also provides oversight and coordination of all federal equal employment opportunity regulations, practices, and policies.

Other federal laws, not enforced by EEOC, also prohibit discrimination and reprisal against federal employees and applicants. The Civil Service Reform Act of 1978 (CSRA) contains a number of prohibitions, known as prohibited personnel practices, which are designed to promote overall fairness in federal personnel actions. 5 U.S.C. 2302. The CSRA prohibits any employee who has authority to take certain personnel actions from discriminating for or against employees or applicants for employment on the bases of race, color, national origin, religion, sex, age or disability. It also provides that certain personnel actions can not be based on attributes or conduct that do not adversely affect employee performance, such as marital status and political affiliation. The Office of Personnel Management (OPM) has interpreted the prohibition of discrimination based on conduct to include discrimination based on sexual orientation. The CSRA also prohibits reprisal against federal employees or applicants for whistle-blowing, or for exercising an appeal, complaint, or grievance right. The CSRA is enforced by both the Office of Special Counsel (OSC) and the Merit Systems Protection Board (MSPB).

Additional information about the enforcement of the CSRA may be found on the OPM web site at http://www.opm.gov/er/address2/guide01.htm; from OSC at (202) 653-7188 or at http://www.osc.gov; and from MSPB at (202) 653-6772 or at http://www.mspb.gov .

Discriminatory Practices

II. What Discriminatory Practices Are Prohibited by These Laws?

Under Title VII, the ADA, and the ADEA, it is illegal to discriminate in any aspect of employment, including:

- hiring and firing;
- compensation, assignment, or classification of employees;
- transfer, promotion, layoff, or recall;
- job advertisements;
- recruitment;
- testing;
- use of company facilities;
- training and apprenticeship programs;
- fringe benefits;
- pay, retirement plans, and disability leave; or
- other terms and conditions of employment.

Discriminatory practices under these laws also include:

- harassment on the basis of race, color, religion, sex, national origin, disability, or age;
- retaliation against an individual for filing a charge of discrimination, participating in an investigation, or opposing discriminatory practices;
- employment decisions based on stereotypes or assumptions about the abilities, traits, or performance of individuals of a certain sex, race, age, religion, or ethnic group, or individuals with disabilities; and
- denying employment opportunities to a person because of marriage to, or association with, an individual of a particular race, religion, national origin, or an individual with a disability. Title VII also prohibits discrimination because of participation in schools or places of worship associated with a particular racial, ethnic, or religious group.

Employers are required to post notices to all employees advising them of their rights under the laws EEOC enforces and their right to be free from retaliation. Such notices must be accessible, as needed, to persons with visual or other disabilities that affect reading.

Note: Many states and municipalities also have enacted protections against discrimination and harassment based on sexual orientation, status as a parent, marital status and political affiliation. For information, please contact the EEOC District Office nearest you.

III. What Other Practices Are Discriminatory Under These Laws?

Title VII

Title VII prohibits not only intentional discrimination, but also practices that have the effect of discriminating against individuals because of their race, color, national origin, religion, or sex.

National Origin Discrimination

- It is illegal to discriminate against an individual because of birthplace, ancestry, culture, or linguistic characteristics common to a specific ethnic group.
- A rule requiring that employees speak only English on the job may violate Title VII unless an employer shows that the requirement is necessary for conducting business. If the employer believes such a rule is necessary, employees must be informed when English is required and the consequences for violating the rule.

The Immigration Reform and Control Act (IRCA) of 1986 requires employers to assure that employees hired are legally authorized to work in the U.S. However, an employer who requests employment verification only for individuals of a particular national origin, or individuals who appear to be or sound foreign, may violate both Title VII and IRCA; verification must be obtained from all applicants and employees. Employers who impose citizenship requirements or give preferences to U.S. citizens in hiring or employment opportunities also may violate IRCA.

Additional information about IRCA may be obtained from the Office of Special Counsel for Immigration-Related Unfair Employment Practices at 1-800-255-7688 (voice), 1-800-237-2515 (TTY for employees/applicants) or 1-800-362-2735 (TTY for employers) or at http://www.usdoj.gov/crt/osc.

Religious Accommodation

- An employer is required to reasonably accommodate the religious belief of an employee or prospective employee, unless doing so would impose an undue hardship.

Sex Discrimination

Title VII's broad prohibitions against sex discrimination specifically cover:

- Sexual Harassment - This includes practices ranging from direct requests for sexual favors to workplace conditions that create a hostile environment for persons of either gender, including same sex harassment. (The "hostile environment" standard also applies to harassment on the bases of race, color, national origin, religion, age, and disability.)
- Pregnancy Based Discrimination - Pregnancy, childbirth, and related medical conditions must be treated in the same way as other temporary illnesses or conditions.

Additional rights are available to parents and others under the Family and Medical Leave Act (FMLA), which is enforced by the U.S. Department of Labor. For information on the FMLA, or to file an FMLA complaint, individuals should contact the nearest office of the Wage and Hour Division, Employment Standards Administration, U.S. Department of Labor. The Wage and Hour Division is listed in most telephone directories under U.S. Government, Department of Labor or at http://www.dol.gov/esa/public/whd_org.htm.

Age Discrimination in Employment Act

The ADEA's broad ban against age discrimination also specifically prohibits:

- statements or specifications in job notices or advertisements of age preference and limitations. An age limit may only be specified in the rare circumstance where age has been proven to be a *bona fide* occupational qualification (BFOQ);
- discrimination on the basis of age by apprenticeship programs, including joint labor-management apprenticeship programs; and
- denial of benefits to older employees. An employer may reduce benefits based on age only if the cost of providing the reduced benefits to older workers is the same as the cost of providing benefits to younger workers.

Equal Pay Act

The EPA prohibits discrimination on the basis of sex in the payment of wages or benefits, where men and women perform work of similar skill, effort, and responsibility for the same employer under similar working conditions.

Note that:

- Employers may not reduce wages of either sex to equalize pay between men and women.
- A violation of the EPA may occur where a different wage was/is paid to a person who worked in the same job before or after an employee of the opposite sex.
- A violation may also occur where a labor union causes the employer to violate the law.

Titles I and V of the Americans with Disabilities Act

The ADA prohibits discrimination on the basis of disability in all employment practices. It is necessary to understand several important ADA definitions to know who is protected by the law and what constitutes illegal discrimination:

Individual with a Disability

> An individual with a disability under the ADA is a person who has a physical or mental impairment that substantially limits one or more major life activities, has a record of such an impairment, or is regarded as having such an impairment. Major life activities are activities that an average person can perform with little or no difficulty such as walking, breathing, seeing, hearing, speaking, learning, and working.

Qualified Individual with a Disability

> A qualified employee or applicant with a disability is someone who satisfies skill, experience, education, and other job-related requirements of the position held or desired, and who, with or without reasonable accommodation, can perform the essential functions of that position.

Reasonable Accommodation

> Reasonable accommodation may include, but is not limited to, making existing facilities used by employees readily accessible to and usable by persons with disabilities; job restructuring; modification of work schedules; providing additional unpaid leave; reassignment to a vacant position; acquiring or modifying equipment or devices; adjusting or modifying examinations, training materials, or policies; and providing qualified readers or interpreters. Reasonable accommodation may be necessary to apply for a job, to perform job functions, or to enjoy the benefits and privileges of employment that are enjoyed by people without disabilities. An employer is not required to lower production standards to make an accommodation. An employer generally is not obligated to provide personal use items such as eyeglasses or hearing aids.

Undue Hardship

> An employer is required to make a reasonable accommodation to a qualified individual with a disability unless doing so would impose an undue hardship on the operation of the employer's business. Undue hardship means an action that requires significant difficulty or expense when considered in relation to

factors such as a business' size, financial resources, and the nature and structure of its operation.

Prohibited Inquiries and Examinations

Before making an offer of employment, an employer may not ask job applicants about the existence, nature, or severity of a disability. Applicants may be asked about their ability to perform job functions. A job offer may be conditioned on the results of a medical examination, but only if the examination is required for all entering employees in the same job category. Medical examinations of employees must be job-related and consistent with business necessity.

Drug and Alcohol Use

Employees and applicants currently engaging in the illegal use of drugs are not protected by the ADA when an employer acts on the basis of such use. Tests for illegal use of drugs are not considered medical examinations and, therefore, are not subject to the ADA's restrictions on medical examinations. Employers may hold individuals who are illegally using drugs and individuals with alcoholism to the same standards of performance as other employees.

The Civil Rights Act of 1991

The Civil Rights Act of 1991 made major changes in the federal laws against employment discrimination enforced by EEOC. Enacted in part to reverse several Supreme Court decisions that limited the rights of persons protected by these laws, the Act also provides additional protections. The Act authorizes compensatory and punitive damages in cases of intentional discrimination, and provides for obtaining attorneys' fees and the possibility of jury trials. It also directs the EEOC to expand its technical assistance and outreach activities.

Employers And Other Entities Covered By EEO Laws

IV. Which Employers and Other Entities Are Covered by These Laws?

Title VII and the ADA cover all private employers, state and local governments, and education institutions that employ 15 or more individuals. These laws also cover private and public employment agencies, labor organizations, and joint labor management committees controlling apprenticeship and training.

The ADEA covers all private employers with 20 or more employees, state and local governments (including school districts), employment agencies and labor organizations.

The EPA covers all employers who are covered by the Federal Wage and Hour Law (the Fair Labor Standards Act). Virtually all employers are subject to the provisions of this Act.

Title VII, the ADEA, and the EPA also cover the federal government. In addition, the federal government is covered by Sections 501 and 505 of the Rehabilitation Act of 1973, as amended, which incorporate the requirements of the ADA. However, different procedures are used for processing complaints of federal discrimination. For more information on how to file a complaint of federal discrimination, contact the EEO office of the federal agency where the alleged discrimination occurred.

The CSRA (not enforced by EEOC) covers most federal agency employees except employees of a government corporation, the Federal Bureau of Investigation, the Central Intelligence Agency, the Defense Intelligence Agency, the National Security Agency, and as determined by the President, any executive agency or unit thereof, the principal function of which is the conduct of foreign intelligence or counterintelligence activities, or the General Accounting Office.

The EEOC'S Charge Processing Procedures

Federal employees or applicants for employment should see the fact sheet about <u>Federal Sector Equal Employment Opportunity Complaint Processing.</u>

V. Who Can File a Charge of Discrimination?

- Any individual who believes that his or her employment rights have been violated may file a charge of discrimination with EEOC.
- In addition, an individual, organization, or agency may file a charge on behalf of another person in order to protect the aggrieved person's identity.

VI. How Is a Charge of Discrimination Filed?

- A charge may be filed by mail or in person at the nearest EEOC office. Individuals may consult their local telephone directory (U.S. Government listing) or call 1-800-669-4000 (voice) or 1-800-669-6820 (TTY) to contact the nearest EEOC office for more information on specific procedures for filing a charge.
- Individuals who need an accommodation in order to file a charge (*e.g.*, sign language interpreter, print materials in an accessible format) should inform the EEOC field office so appropriate arrangements can be made.
- Federal employees or applicants for employment should see the fact sheet about <u>Federal Sector Equal Employment Opportunity Complaint Processing.</u>

VII. What Information Must Be Provided to File a Charge?

- The complaining party's name, address, and telephone number;
- The name, address, and telephone number of the respondent employer, employment agency, or union that is alleged to have discriminated, and number of employees (or union members), if known;
- A short description of the alleged violation (the event that caused the complaining party to believe that his or her rights were violated); and
- The date(s) of the alleged violation(s).
- Federal employees or applicants for employment should see the fact sheet about Federal Sector Equal Employment Opportunity Complaint Processing.

VIII. What Are the Time Limits for Filing a Charge of Discrimination?

All laws enforced by EEOC, except the Equal Pay Act, require filing a charge with EEOC before a private lawsuit may be filed in court. There are strict time limits within which charges must be filed:

- A charge must be filed with EEOC within 180 days from the date of the alleged violation, in order to protect the charging party's rights.
- This 180-day filing deadline is extended to 300 days if the charge also is covered by a state or local anti-discrimination law. For ADEA charges, only state laws extend the filing limit to 300 days.
- These time limits do not apply to claims under the Equal Pay Act, because under that Act persons do not have to first file a charge with EEOC in order to have the right to go to court. However, since many EPA claims also raise Title VII sex discrimination issues, it may be advisable to file charges under both laws within the time limits indicated.
- To protect legal rights, it is always best to contact EEOC promptly when discrimination is suspected.
- Federal employees or applicants for employment should see the fact sheet about Federal Sector Equal Employment Opportunity Complaint Processing.

IX. What Agency Handles a Charge that is also Covered by State or Local Law?

Many states and localities have anti-discrimination laws and agencies responsible for enforcing those laws. EEOC refers to these agencies as "Fair Employment Practices Agencies (FEPAs)." Through the use of "work sharing agreements," EEOC and the FEPAs avoid duplication of effort while at the same time ensuring that a charging party's rights are protected under both federal and state law.

- If a charge is filed with a FEPA and is also covered by federal law, the FEPA "dual files" the charge with EEOC to protect federal rights. The charge usually will be retained by the FEPA for handling.

- If a charge is filed with EEOC and also is covered by state or local law, EEOC "dual files" the charge with the state or local FEPA, but ordinarily retains the charge for handling.

X. What Happens after a Charge is Filed with EEOC?

The employer is notified that the charge has been filed. From this point there are a number of ways a charge may be handled:

- A charge may be assigned for priority investigation if the initial facts appear to support a violation of law. When the evidence is less strong, the charge may be assigned for follow up investigation to determine whether it is likely that a violation has occurred.
- EEOC can seek to settle a charge at any stage of the investigation if the charging party and the employer express an interest in doing so. If settlement efforts are not successful, the investigation continues.
- In investigating a charge, EEOC may make written requests for information, interview people, review documents, and, as needed, visit the facility where the alleged discrimination occurred. When the investigation is complete, EEOC will discuss the evidence with the charging party or employer, as appropriate.
- The charge may be selected for EEOC's mediation program if both the charging party and the employer express an interest in this option. Mediation is offered as an alternative to a lengthy investigation. Participation in the mediation program is confidential, voluntary, and requires consent from both charging party and employer. If mediation is unsuccessful, the charge is returned for investigation.
- A charge may be dismissed at any point if, in the agency's best judgment, further investigation will not establish a violation of the law. A charge may be dismissed at the time it is filed, if an initial in-depth interview does not produce evidence to support the claim. When a charge is dismissed, a notice is issued in accordance with the law which gives the charging party 90 days in which to file a lawsuit on his or her own behalf.
- Federal employees or applicants for employment should see the fact sheet about Federal Sector Equal Employment Opportunity Complaint Processing.

XI. How Does EEOC Resolve Discrimination Charges?

- If the evidence obtained in an investigation does not establish that discrimination occurred, this will be explained to the charging party. A required notice is then issued, closing the case and giving the charging party 90 days in which to file a lawsuit on his or her own behalf.
- If the evidence establishes that discrimination has occurred, the employer and the charging party will be informed of this in a letter of determination

that explains the finding. EEOC will then attempt conciliation with the employer to develop a remedy for the discrimination.

- If the case is successfully conciliated, or if a case has earlier been successfully mediated or settled, neither EEOC nor the charging party may go to court unless the conciliation, mediation, or settlement agreement is not honored.
- If EEOC is unable to successfully conciliate the case, the agency will decide whether to bring suit in federal court. If EEOC decides not to sue, it will issue a notice closing the case and giving the charging party 90 days in which to file a lawsuit on his or her own behalf. In Title VII and ADA cases against state or local governments, the Department of Justice takes these actions.
- Federal employees or applicants for employment should see the fact sheet about <u>Federal Sector Equal Employment Opportunity Complaint Processing.</u>

XII. When Can an Individual File an Employment Discrimination Lawsuit in Court?

A charging party may file a lawsuit within 90 days after receiving a notice of a "right to sue" from EEOC, as stated above. Under Title VII and the ADA, a charging party also can request a notice of "right to sue" from EEOC 180 days after the charge was first filed with the Commission, and may then bring suit within 90 days after receiving this notice. Under the ADEA, a suit may be filed at any time 60 days after filing a charge with EEOC, but not later than 90 days after EEOC gives notice that it has completed action on the charge.

Under the EPA, a lawsuit must be filed within two years (three years for willful violations) of the discriminatory act, which in most cases is payment of a discriminatory lower wage.

Federal employees or applicants for employment should see the fact sheet about <u>Federal Sector Equal Employment Opportunity Complaint Processing.</u>

XIII. What Remedies Are Available When Discrimination Is Found?

The "relief" or remedies available for employment discrimination, whether caused by intentional acts or by practices that have a discriminatory effect, may include:

- back pay,
- hiring,
- promotion,
- reinstatement,
- front pay,
- reasonable accommodation, or

- other actions that will make an individual "whole" (in the condition s/he would have been but for the discrimination).

Remedies also may include payment of:

- attorneys' fees,
- expert witness fees, and
- court costs.

Under most EEOC-enforced laws, compensatory and punitive damages also may be available where intentional discrimination is found. Damages may be available to compensate for actual monetary losses, for future monetary losses, and for mental anguish and inconvenience. Punitive damages also may be available if an employer acted with malice or reckless indifference. Punitive damages are not available against the federal, state or local governments.

In cases concerning reasonable accommodation under the ADA, compensatory or punitive damages may not be awarded to the charging party if an employer can demonstrate that "good faith" efforts were made to provide reasonable accommodation.

An employer may be required to post notices to all employees addressing the violations of a specific charge and advising them of their rights under the laws EEOC enforces and their right to be free from retaliation. Such notices must be accessible, as needed, to persons with visual or other disabilities that affect reading.

The employer also may be required to take corrective or preventive actions to cure the source of the identified discrimination and minimize the chance of its recurrence, as well as discontinue the specific discriminatory practices involved in the case.

The Commission

XIV. What Is EEOC and How Does It Operate?

EEOC is an independent federal agency originally created by Congress in 1964 to enforce Title VII of the Civil Rights Act of 1964. The Commission is composed of five Commissioners and a General Counsel appointed by the President and confirmed by the Senate. Commissioners are appointed for five-year staggered terms; the General Counsel's term is four years. The President designates a Chair and a Vice-Chair. The Chair is the chief executive officer of the Commission. The Commission has authority to establish equal employment policy and to approve litigation. The General Counsel is responsible for conducting litigation.

EEOC carries out its enforcement, education and technical assistance activities through 50 field offices serving every part of the nation.

The nearest EEOC field office may be contacted by calling: 1-800-669-4000 (voice) or 1-800-669-6820 (TTY).

Information And Assistance Available From EEOC

XV. What Information and Other Assistance Is Available from EEOC?

EEOC provides a range of informational materials and assistance to individuals and entities with rights and responsibilities under EEOC-enforced laws. Most materials and assistance are provided to the public at no cost. Additional specialized training and technical assistance are provided on a fee basis under the auspices of the EEOC Education, Technical Assistance, and Training Revolving Fund Act of 1992. For information on educational and other assistance available, contact the nearest EEOC office by calling: 1-800-669-4000 (voice) or 1-800-669-6820 (TTY).

Publications available at no cost include posters advising employees of their EEO rights, and pamphlets, manuals, fact sheets, and enforcement guidance on laws enforced by the Commission. For a list of EEOC publications, or to order publications, write, call, or fax:

U.S. Equal Employment Opportunity Commission
Publications Distribution Center
P.O. Box 12549
Cincinnati, Ohio 45212-0549
1-800-669-3362 (voice)
1-800-800-3302 (TTY)
513-489-8692 (fax)

Telephone operators are available to take orders (in English or Spanish) from 8:30 a.m. to 5:00 p.m. (EST), Monday through Friday. Orders generally are mailed within 48 hours after receipt.

Information about EEOC and the laws it enforces also can be found at the following internet address: http://www.eeoc.gov.